# a concealed GOD

RELIGION,
SCIENCE,
AND THE
SEARCH
FOR TRUTH

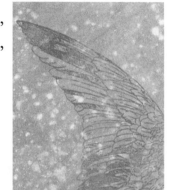

*a concealed*
GOD

STEFAN EINHORN

Translated from the Swedish by Linda Schenck

TEMPLETON FOUNDATION PRESS
PHILADELPHIA AND LONDON

Templeton Foundation Press
Five Radnor Corporate Center, Suite 120
100 Matsonford Road
Radnor, Pennsylvania 19087

Designed and typeset by Gopa  & Ted2
Printed by Sheridan Books

Scripture quotations are from the TANAKH published by The
Jewish Publication Society of America (1917) and *The New
Revised Standard Version* of the Bible © 1989 by the Division of
Christian Education of the National Council of the Churches of
Christ in the United States of America.

Library of Congress Cataloging-in-Publication Data
Einhorn, Stefan.
  [En dold Gud. English]
  A concealed God : religion, science, and the search for truth /
Stefan Einhorn ; translated from the Swedish by Linda Schenck.
      p. cm.
Includes bibliographical references and index.
  ISBN 1-890151-93-9 (alk. paper)
  1. Theism. 2.  Hidden God. 3.  Religion and science. 4.  Religions.
I. Title.
  BL200 .E3713 2002
  291.2'11—dc21

                                        2002003981

Printed in the United States of America

02  03  04  05  06  07      10 9 8 7 6 5 4 3 2 1

Every concept of God is a mere simulacrum, a false likeness,
an idol: it could not reveal God himself.
—Gregory of Nyssa, Christian mystic

It is other than all that is known. It is above the unknown.
—Hindu text

Of this there is no academic proof in the world;
For it is hidden, and hidden, and hidden.
—Jalaluddin Rumi, Sufi mystic

No words can describe it. No example can point to it.
—Dudjom Rinpoche, Buddhist spiritual guide

I have not seen Thee, yet I tell Thy praise,
Nor known Thee, yet I image forth thy ways.
—Jewish mystic

The Tao that can be expressed is not the eternal Tao.
—*Tao Te Ching*

If we start from our human scale of existence and explore
the content of the Universe further and further, we finally arrive,
both in the large and in the small, at misty distances where
first our senses and then even our concepts fail us.
—Emil Wiechert, scientist

"Goodbye," said the fox. "And now here is my secret,
a very simple secret: It is only with the heart that one can
see rightly; what is essential is invisible to the eye."
—Antoine de Saint-Exupéry, *The Little Prince*

*To Damiki*

~

# Contents

## ~ Acknowledgments

A NUMBER OF PEOPLE have helped me with the manuscript of this book, with suggestions and criticisms as well as with encouragement and support. I am deeply indebted to them all, and would particularly like to mention a few.

Firstly, Dr. Rigmor Robèrt, whose knowledge and wisdom have been of indispensable support throughout the journey, from the initial idea to the submitted manuscript, and for bringing me to the insight that it is permissible to regard life as a mystery.

Associate Professor Per Beskow, Imam Abd-al-Haqq Kielan, Professor Charles Kurland, Rabbi Morton Narrowe, Professor Peter Schalk, Anna Smidhammar, B.A., and Associate Professor Farkas Vanky have all read, checked the facts, and expressed their views on selected parts of the manuscript. I am most grateful to them for this assistance, and take this opportunity to emphasize that I, as author, bear sole responsibility for the contents of this book.

I am grateful to Linda Schenck for translating this book into English and for fruitful, rewarding collaboration.

Susanne Einhorn has supported me unreservedly throughout my work, and has enthusiastically read various versions of the manuscript. Looking back at the earliest drafts, I can only feel blushing amazement at her initial enthusiasm, and gratitude to her for not having let on. I am also grateful to Anette and Reuben Sallmander for their friendship and support.

In addition, I would like to thank my colleagues at work for being there for me and for enabling me to study the subject and write this book.

On a personal note: at some time in our lives, we may experience the collapse of all that is rational and commonsensical, and find ourselves faced with the incomprehensible. When the moment passes, we may choose to believe we were being duped by our emotions, or to trust in the truth of that passing feeling. I decided to believe that the experience may have contained a kernel of truth, and this book is a result of that decision.

*a concealed* GOD

## ◌ Introduction

*It is said that during World War II, inside Auschwitz, a group of religious Jews who had experienced the horrors committed in the concentration camp decided to put God on trial. There were counsels for the prosecution and the defense, a judge and a jury. When it was time to pronounce judgment there was total unanimity: God was found guilty. Court adjourned, with the announcement that it was time for evening prayers.*
—based on a text by Elie Wiesel

SKEPTICS REFER TO GOD as a creation of humankind. They hold that people require a father figure, a conscience, a source of solace, and a pledge of eternal life in order to function. They refer to the work of scientists, who have now solved many of the riddles of existence that could previously only be explained by invoking an unknown force in the universe, as proof that the term "God" no longer fills a function. We are, skeptics say, alone in an immense universe that once upon a time and quite by chance gave rise to the preconditions for the origin of life. This may be true.

On the other hand, it may be the case that there is a concealed force in the universe; a force that can be experienced but cannot be described. Could it be that our existence—our lives and our deaths—have some higher meaning, and that this "Other" is neither accessible to our senses nor to scientific methods? Could religions be correct in their dogged persistence that the divine exists?

Religions may be right, but about what? There are many more notions about the meaning of the word "God" than there are religions on our earth. Since we are unable to describe God in words, imagery, myths, and symbols have been developed to give us some sense of what the divine represents. In this way, God may be compared with natural phenomena such as the sun or the heavens, or with representations in our world, such as a judge or a father. Other descriptions of the divine include the Great Mother (in the shape of the earth), the mother of us all. Originally, these symbols and myths were used as attempts to describe that which defies description. Over time, these figures of speech have come to have lives of their own. Symbols and myths, the original functions of which were to disseminate emotional insights and make the divine comprehensible to the mind, have been transformed into absolute truths. Some of these have come to dominate entire religions.

And so today, if we compare descriptions of the divine in different religions they appear more or less contradictory. Some religions assert that God can appear in the guise of a human being, others assure us that the divine could not possibly take on human shape. According to some religions, God has personal attributes, while according to others the divine can have no human characteristics. These differences have led many religions to claim that theirs is the *only* true knowledge of the divine, that only they have the right to the truth. For this and several other reasons the "truths" of religions seem both antithetical and irrational to many contemporary human beings.

Many of us find it more and more difficult to keep our bearings among the many rites and traditions of religious institutions as we grow increasingly skeptical of an idea of God that cannot be reconciled with reason. Thus, over time, fewer and fewer people in the Western world have come to practice a religion. Many deny the existence of a God, or see questions about God as unanswerable. Others believe in God, but describe their faith as outside any established religion; the New Age movement is one such expression. Others turn to Eastern religions that offer other varieties of spiritual searching. Sometimes the term "God" is deprived of its spiritual dimension altogether, and used as a representation of human characteristics, such as "our inner strength" or "an inner moral code."

In our societies, religion as a means of coming into contact with the divine is a weaker force today than in the past, and at the same time religions are becoming stultified around their symbols and descriptions of a "humanoid" God. More and more people experience a sense of disorientation and emptiness in an existence no longer rooted in the great mysteries. Lama Anagarika Govinda, a Buddhist writer, has said that even the deepest statements of religion are worthless if they cannot be re-experienced. Although one might imagine that it is the political power, external ornamentation, number of believers, social network, or laws of religions that determine their significance, in the long run the value and strength of religions are determined more by their inner truth and their ability to disseminate this message to the hearts of individual human beings.

Must we abandon our faith in God if we have rejected the gray-bearded father figure of our childhoods? Must we abstain from belief in God because we perceive the irreconcilable aspects of different religions? Possibly not. Perhaps we can behave as scientists do when they have run a series of experiments only to obtain contradictory results. They ask themselves whether there might not be a unifying, logical, overarching conclusion that binds all the results together and leads to the most probable explanation. If we apply this question to the divine, we may phrase it as follows: *What unites the apparently antithetical systems of thought that characterize religions?*

The answer may be formulated in many ways, but it always appears to contain one common denominator. What unites all religions is that they refer to an indescribable force they claim to be the basis of existence and the inner core of faith, a force we all carry with us at the depths of our being. It has many different names and designations. I have chosen to call this force "a concealed God."

This book explores the questions of whether there is a concealed God and whether this concept of God links different religions together. Has belief in God been transformed into an insoluble paradox now that scientific progress has solved mysteries previous generations could only explain by referring to the divine? Has our newly accumulated knowledge about humankind, our world, and our universe made the concept of God superfluous? Or is the existence of a concealed God both real and reconcilable with all the knowledge about human beings and nature we have attained over the last few centuries?

If we believe there is in fact a concealed God that links different religions together, then we find ourselves faced with another question. If an indescribable, concealed God is the central theme of the various religions, how can we ever arrive at and understand this concept of God? Is it possible to make manifest that which is concealed?

In response to the universal, human striving to find the highest truth, all religions have developed methods for pursuing the inner search by which we may attempt to establish contact with the divine. These paths are not easy to travel: they demand time, motivation, and hard work, but they are there, and the road maps have been preserved.

There is an endless supply of literature about the divine. Religions offer books and articles galore. Philosophy, psychology, and the natural sciences have also produced enormous quantities of material that may give us knowledge about religion, and about the question of whether there is a God. No human being could possibly read all that has been written about the divine in a single lifetime. The wide range of this discipline makes it difficult to see in its entirety and a challenge to interpret. The diversity of cultures, epochs, and languages poses an added problem, since misapprehensions and simplifications readily arise. Moreover, it is impossible to be perfectly objective in relation to a matter that is fundamentally subjective and indescribable. A written record is colored by the personal interpretations of the author and his or her sampling of the range of existing documentation.

For all these reasons, this book is no more than my personal attempt to summarize certain aspects of what unifies different religions' descriptions of the concealed God and the paths to the divine, as well as the question of whether this concept of God can be reconciled with scientific, rational thought. It spans a wide scope, and I hope for the reader's indulgence with regard to anything I may have neglected or misinterpreted.

Religious belief may have a value of its own and does not necessarily need to be subjected to rational analysis. In a culture dominated by reason, perhaps religious systems should be declared protected zones. Since religion has lost much of its clout in Western societies, however, it is interesting to note that people seem less and less inclined to accept a religion that does not seek support in reason. I myself was schooled in scientific thought, and therefore my ambition has been to allow reason to permeate my thinking and writing about things that cannot be proven, always aware of the fact that religious belief must, to some extent, be a matter of faith.

It has been my constant ambition to avoid complex explanations when answering questions about the natural sciences and I have attempted to do so in this book as well. At times I may have oversimplified, but perhaps when dealing with a subject that is fundamentally indescribable and beyond words, it is impossible not to do so.

Books need not necessarily be read from cover to cover. In this one, some sections may interest some readers, while others may find other parts attractive. One way of reading this book might be to begin with the final, more general, section—"A Concealed God?"—and then return to focus on other parts.

Why is the question of God important? As I see it, there are a few fundamental elements that make the existence of God a significant issue for humankind. The first is that religions, as a rule, describe the divine as the core of our existence. If there is a God, we are participants in a plan we cannot embrace using our everyday thought processes. Alternatively, if there is not a God, this is also of fundamental importance. Without a God, we are entirely in control of our own lives, human existence, and the destiny of our world.

Another reason is that many people today are not finding what they are looking for within the framework their religion has to offer. Many refrain from believing in the existence of a God when they can no longer make their adult intellects accept a simplified notion of the divine. The rationalist stance has come to replace belief in the divine, and a person with no spiritual context may feel lost and insecure, living in a world apparently without meaning or purpose.

The question is whether there might still be some truth, a notion of God at the center of all religions that could awaken our spirituality and the sense of mystery in us. This may be a feeling we need of a mystery we will never be able entirely to solve. It is related to a belief in the value of life and to a search that can provide our existence with direction and purpose.

There is one other important reason why the question of God is a central one. Developments in science and technology have been extraordinarily rapid over the last few centuries and there is no indication that this trend has peaked. Today, we have found cures for many of the diseases that formerly caused great suffering and many deaths. Most people in the Western world do not face starvation, and the standard of living has continued to rise. We work less and have more time to use as we please. In this light, the opportunities for happiness ought to be improving.

At the same time, developments in technology and the sciences have put our earth at great peril. Weapons of mass destruction, environmental degradation, and new epidemics may ultimately result in the extinction of the human race. We all know what may happen, but for some strange reason we have not been able to bring the self-destructive forces to a halt. In pivotal times like ours, many people seek counsel and an ethical structure to hold onto. I wonder whether perhaps we can find the wisdom we so desperately need at the core of religion, in the force we refer to as God.

*Part I*

## On God and Religions

# ᨀ 1

## *What Is a Religion?*

T HERE ARE MANY theories about the origins of religion. Some of the important initial functions of religions probably included helping human beings to seek what may be called the spiritual or the divine, revealing that which is beyond the world of the senses and trying to explain the mysteries of existence. Over time, religions have taken on more and more functions and as a result their structures have become increasingly complex. The various aspects of religion might be systematized as follows:

+ rites, traditions, and myths;
+ moral/ethical values;
+ comfort and caring;
+ social systems;
+ spiritual (divine) content.

Considering these varied functions, as well as the fact that the different faiths are dissimilar in many respects, we can see there is no simple, single definition of "religion." However, I offer this possible one: *A system of thought attempting to provide an understanding of that which cannot be experienced through the human senses and the rational mind.*

When we compare the religions of the world, we can see both differences and similarities. It is not only that their traditions and rituals vary; there are also major discrepancies with regard to how they treat notions like "the human soul," "the afterlife," and "the divine." At the same time, it is no understatement to say that some of the similarities are very striking indeed.

## RITES, TRADITIONS, AND MYTHS

Rites, traditions, and myths are the external forms of expressions of religion. Religions have developed these expressions for many reasons:

+ As symbolic manifestations of the divine. Divine reality is fundamentally indescribable and can only be experienced emotionally, which is one explanation of why religious rites are so often emotionally charged. Symbols thus become tools by way of which we may experience the innermost truths and a God beyond words.
+ To create a sense of belonging within a people or religious grouping. This strengthens individual identity and the feeling of being part of something larger than oneself, not only in relation to contemporary practitioners of the religion but also in relation to all those who have practiced it before them.
+ As an attempt to achieve influence over that which is beyond our control.
+ As a constant reminder of religion and the divine.
+ To instill a sense of respect and humility and give emotional insight into our being part of a larger context.
+ Like art, to provide positive experiences through the senses.
+ As a form of pedagogy. Traditions, rites, and narratives save each generation from having to begin all over.

While there are innumerable variations, similar narratives, rites, and customs appear across many religions. Sometimes religions with origins in completely different parts of the world, independent of one another, turn out to have developed similar myths and rites.

The creation myth, for one, is similarly structured in a number of religions. Several describe the universe and humankind as having been created by the gods out of the body of either a giant or a monster. In Old Norse mythology, Ymer, a giant, is killed and the world created from his body. In the ancient Vedic hymn, we find the story of Purusha, the primal man, out of whose body the universe was created. In the *Enuma elish*, the Babylonian myth of creation, Tiamat, the "only sea," is killed, and heaven and earth created out of her body.

The original sea, the water out of which the divinity created the world by structuring what once was nothing but chaos, is a recurrent theme in other religions as well. For instance, in the story of creation in the Hebrew scriptures we may read how, on the first day, "the earth was a formless void and darkness covered the face of the deep, while a wind from God swept over the face of the waters" (Genesis 1:2).

The flood—a terrible storm near the beginning of time that threatens to drown all living things—is another common mythological theme. In both the biblical story of Noah and the Babylonian Gilgamesh epic the protagonist builds a boat in which animals and human beings survive the flood, thus saving life on earth. Indian and Greek mythologies also have similar tales.

Likewise, many religions have similar rites, although these may have very different interpretations. The meaning of one and the same rite may change over time, mean different things in different religions, or have varying functions in different schools within the same faith. The rite of purification, for example, occurs in a number of religions and has a variety of meanings. In Christianity, baptism signifies becoming a member of the church, and symbolizes death and subsequent resurrection. The ritual bath or *mikve* in conjunction with conversion to Judaism also symbolizes death and rebirth. Women also have a mikve before weddings, after menstrual periods, and after childbirth, but in this context the mikve symbolizes a restoration of spiritual purity, like the male mikve before the Sabbath and high holy days. In other traditions, the cleansing process takes the form of a life-giving or healing rite.

Rites with identical concepts that can be found in various religious systems include those around birth, initiation, the new year, marriage ceremonies, and funerals. Clearly, rituals of emotional commitment are the practical backbone of many religions. Many of these rites have probably lost their original significance, only to have a new meaning attached to them.

Prayer is a kind of rite found in many religious systems, although with different expressions and aims. Prayer may be a way of communicating with the divine in order to ask for comfort, aid, or support in everyday life. In relation to this function, prayer may be more or less ritualized, sometimes in the form of religious services. Prayer may also function as part of the inner search for spiritual experience and knowledge about the innermost truths. In this dimension, prayer can take the form of meditation and contemplation.

Religious traditions have long been passed down from one generation to the next in written form. Such traditions may be commandments or norms, or absolute truths, known as dogmas. The dogmas found in different religions may be contradictory in their basic respects.

The rites, traditions, and myths of different religions can thus have shared features that can be interpreted as pointing toward a common inner truth. At the same time, these external expressions of religions can differ greatly. To some extent, this may be explained by the fact that they developed in different cultures.

## MORAL/ETHICAL VALUES

*Two things fill the mind with ever increasing wonder and awe the more
often and the more intensely the mind of thought is drawn to them:
the starry heavens above me and the moral law within me.*

—Immanuel Kant (1724–1804)

All the major religions, irrespective of the way their rites, traditions, and spiritual content differ, have a foundation in moral and ethical values. The basic "golden rule" found in many religions, with only small variations on the theme, is that we should treat others as we wish to be treated ourselves. Love of one's fellow human beings, compassion, doing good deeds, and refraining from evil are key values in these ethical systems. Within them, there are a number of specific laws and norms, such as a general prohibition against murder, thievery, and lying. Some religions also regulate more mundane activities.

It may seem remarkable that different religions, including some that had no means of being in close contact, could develop similar moral and ethical principles. There are several possible explanations for these common systems of moral values, laws, and rules.

+ These systems were created by human beings in order that as many people as possible should have the greatest possible happiness and security. Societies are dependent for their stability on their citizens living in harmony in accordance with norms and laws with detailed regulations. Religion is often one of the main structuring principles in these societies and can therefore be used to maintain the ethical norms.
+ Moral values are innate characteristics. *Homo sapiens* was able to

develop out of other animal species because we acquired properties that favored our ability to survive, including sophisticated brains and the ability to shape tools with our hands. Similarly, animals and human beings may have developed instincts that can prevent us from doing one another harm. Human beings living in groups developed empathy and consideration, which became survival advantages. Theoretically, humanoid species that did not possess these qualities may have destroyed one another and, consequently, themselves. Thus the species that survived had developed the ability to think ethically.

✦ Moral/ethical systems originated in a higher ethical principle, a kind of "moral constitution," expressed through religions. In accordance with this explanation many religions claim that the doing of good deeds and the abstention from doing evil gives rise to positive developments for both the individual and the entire world. Christianity and Islam assert heaven and hell as parts of the system of reward and punishment we will find after death. In Eastern religions a similar system is inherent to the concept of karma. Good deeds generate positive karma, which leads to rewards in this life or a future life, while evil deeds have the corresponding negative consequences.

## COMFORT AND CARING

The development of the human brain has enabled humankind to become increasingly intelligent and thus to understand more and more about the world we live in. At the same time, our ability to consider our existence gives rise to new problems, including anxiety, fear, grief, depression, and worry. We wonder what we are living for, and we may fear death.

One of the missions of religion is to comfort us, to still our worries and our fears. Religion attempts to explain to us why we live and to provide us with answers to the meaning and the aim of existence. It also brings us solace and guidance when we are grieving. Some of these methods we immediately associate with the word "religion." Prayer, penance, and the search for deliverance or insight are all ways of bringing us to inner peace. Other methods are more reminiscent of those of psychotherapy. These include confession and particular forms of meditation. In this respect the representatives of religion sometimes play a therapeutic role.

## SOCIAL SYSTEMS

Religions, like other social systems, have taken on the task of caring for their members. Communities have arisen around religious institutions. They bring people together and protect individuals from feeling too lonely, as well as provide protection for the weak. Systems of providing care for the poor, the elderly, and the sick have developed in these contexts. Religions have also taken on responsibility for other social functions, such as education, weddings, and funerals. In the Western world, as societies have come to take over more of these functions and religions have been deprived of them, these responsibilities have been shifted to the secular authorities. In societies where religious institutions are still strong, or have even taken on governmental powers, these responsibilities have remained more within their sphere of authority.

There are several possible explanations for why religion originally shouldered these responsibilities. One may be that in some societies religion was the primary organization providing coherence, and so these functions, so central to social cohesion, fell to them. Another possible explanation in relation to some but not all religions may be the opportunity to proselytize. Social activities and institutions that care for the sick, the elderly, and the poor may be a way of spreading the message of religion to large groups of people. A third explanation has to do with the message of love that permeates religion. Love of our fellow human beings may be expressed in a desire to help and support the needy.

## THE SPIRITUAL (DIVINE) CONTENT

Spiritual experience is the foundation of religions. Concepts about the divine and about human experience of the divine has remained at their core. In many religions, the idea of "God" is the focus of that spiritual content.

Beliefs about God may take many expressions, even within one and the same religion. Christianity, for instance, speaks of God as a Trinity. The Father designates an aspect of the divine as the creator of the universe. The Son is the aspect of the divine as embodied in Jesus Christ, a human being who walked on earth. The Holy Spirit is a third aspect, unifying

Father and Son and found at the center of the human soul. These three aspects of God are always one single divinity, though separate.

In Hinduism the divine finds expression as a large number of gods, some with overlapping yet distinct missions and forms. At the same time, Hinduism clarifies that these gods are basically all expressions of one and the same God. Other religions, including Buddhism and Taoism, do not use the term "God" as a designation of the Absolute.

Many schools of religion share the notion that the divine exists inside every human being as well as outside, that our inner beings are in direct contact with the Absolute, that the core of each individual is divine. The mystical traditions of the major religions focus on this idea of searching for the divine within us: mystics are usually guided toward insight by intuition and feelings rather than by reason or the senses. The aim of this search is an experience of being in contact or in unity with that which is greater than ourselves. Mystical experience is also often accompanied by a sense of unity with the universe. The means used for the inner search are varied indeed, comprising techniques such as meditation, prayer, and contemplation. The highest insights are achieved gradually, and the search is usually a long one. To many people, the term "mysticism" has an aura of the supernatural or magical, but mysticism actually includes a number of tangible methods aimed at achieving insight.

A theme in several religions is that our conscious experience of the world is really nothing but a pale shadow of true reality. It is in this "real reality" beyond sensory impressions that we can discover the deepest truths and search for the innermost meaning of life, the connection between body and soul, and the knowledge of what may be after death.

## WHY DO RELIGIONS DIFFER?

Could the theses and dogmas of the many religions all possibly be true? No, of course not. Christianity and Hinduism assert that it is possible for a human being to be God. This belief is diametrically opposed to that of Judaism and Islam, which claim that God cannot take on a human form. Judaism believes in the coming of the Messiah, while the central dogma of Christianity is that the Messiah has already walked the earth. Creation myths, too, are contradictory: for instance, the Hindu creation myth is at variance with that of the monotheistic religions. Similarly, it is difficult to reconcile the ideas of Hinduism and Buddhism regarding reincarnation with a belief in the life we live on earth as our only life, and with the picture held by the monotheistic religions of what happens after death. Moreover, there are various religions that accept the existence of other faiths, but still see their own as the only "truth."

A closely related discussion centers on whether God could really have done the things the religious scriptures describe. Take the Bible, for example. Did God really send "a pestilence" causing the deaths of seventy thousand of the people of Israel because King David had decreed that the tribes of Israel and Judah should be numbered (2 Samuel 24, 1 Chronicles 21)? Did God really command that all the Midianites should be killed, including women and children, except for some thirty-two thousand "young girls who have not known a man by sleeping with him" (Numbers 31)? These stories appear more to describe the cruelty of humankind than characteristics of God.

Clearly, the differences and inconsistencies among the scriptures, beliefs, and traditions of all the various religions would suffice to fill several volumes, or perhaps a library. The obvious conclusion is that a great deal of what religion calls eternal truths must be of human invention. Still, there are elements all religions share, including a moral and ethical structure, the idea of a higher reality, a large number of myths and rites, and their social structures. And so we ask: What unites religions with regard to the notion of the divine?

## ～ 2

## *God: What God?*

A s we have seen, religions attribute various qualities and functions to the divine, some of which occur in many religions, some in fewer, and some of which have changed dramatically over time. A list of the qualities and functions religions have assigned to the divine might include:

+ God created the universe and all life.
+ God is omniscient and omnipotent.
+ God is able to affect and make decisions about our lives.
+ God is the basis and prerequisite for everything.
+ We human beings are lost, but God can deliver us.
+ God established the laws that govern good and evil.
+ It is in God's power to determine whether or not our world should go on existing.
+ It is through the divine that wisdom and love are disseminated throughout the world.
+ God established the laws of nature (statements describing a regularity in nature) that govern the universe.
+ God has an impact on what happens to us after death.
+ God can give meaning and content to our lives.
+ God can take part in the creation of the kingdom of God.

The characteristics attributed to the divinity may be ranked on a spectrum ranging from a comprehensible God who thinks human thoughts and has a human appearance at the one extreme to an indescribable, incomprehensible, completely concealed God at the other. God may be like a friend or a fellow human being with whom a devout believer may conduct an inner dialogue. Such a God is immediately accessible to provide solace, intimacy, and advice. To others, God is beyond all human qualities, fully veiled and fundamentally inaccessible to the individual. Between these two extremes, we find many other concepts of God.

Another issue where notions of the divine are polarized is the question of whether or not the divine may be found inside a human being, or whether God exists only outside us. Abstaining from generalizations, we can say that the God to whom human qualities are attributed has a tendency to be associated with an external force, while the concealed aspects of the divine may be referred to as both an internal and external force.

Some religions, including Christianity and Hinduism, claim that a number of these qualities and functions may exist simultaneously in the divine. For instance, God may be indescribable and concealed at the same time as the divine is revealed to humankind, or God may exist as both an external and an internal force. In other religions, such as Islam, the notion of the divine seems more unified.

## GOD IN NATURE

*Thou appearest beautifully on the horizon of heaven, Thou living Aten, the beginning of life....Though thou art in their faces, no one knows thy going.*
—Pharaoh Akhenaten (1375–1345 BCE)

The thought that god(s) exists in the things and the life around us is mainly found in ancient religions, although it is not absent today. Just as a tree or a rock formation may be regarded as possessing a divine soul, animals may also be considered divine, and a statue of a divinity may be regarded as the god. Natural phenomena such as the sun, the moon, thunder, or fire may be portrayed as having divine attributes.

The god of the heavens is a commonly occurring god of nature. The boundary is blurry between the notion of a god dwelling in the heavens (as is also the case in contemporary monotheistic religions) and the idea that a god *is* the heavens. Zeus and Jupiter, worshiped by the classical Greeks and Romans respectively, are two familiar examples of gods of the heavens. The god of the heavens is often said to have created the world.

One of the earliest forms of monotheism took shape over three thousand years ago in Egypt. Pharaoh Akhenaten (1375–1345 BCE) banned the earlier religion with its panoply of gods and decreed instead that his people were to worship the sun, Aten, as the one and only god. Thus, during a short time period, there was monotheistic worship of a natural phenomenon. There is a fascinating hypothesis that this form of monotheism was a source of inspiration for Moses in his further development of Judaism.

Whatever aspect of nature is worshiped is considered sacred and capable of making the spiritual, or the divine, accessible. It is easier to relate to a more comprehensible kind of god than to seek a god who is concealed and inexplicable. The way the Israelites and their priests quickly came to worship a golden calf when their leader vanished up toward the top of Mount Sinai may be seen as one example of the power of attraction exerted by a visible, tangible symbol of the divine.

Pantheism is a more extended expression of the idea that God is in nature: the notion that God and the world are one and indivisible. The world may be described as the "body" of God. Pantheism may also imply that God is the innermost reality and basis of all things, but without necessarily being *identical* with nature. Various contemporary religions contain pantheistic ideas, such as in the following lines from the Hindu Upanishads:

Fire is his head; His eyes, the moon and sun;
The regions of space, His ears; His voice, the revealed Veda;
Fire is his head; His eyes, the moon and sun;
Wind, His breath; His heart, the whole world. Out of His feet,
The earth. Truly, He is the Inner Soul of all.

The Jewish philosopher and mystic Baruch Spinoza (1632–1677) was a representative of monotheistic pantheism. Spinoza believed that God and nature were identical.

## A HUMAN GOD

Many religions contain the idea that a god has wandered the earth in a human shape. Sometimes it bears the designation "incarnation," meaning that for some period of time the god becomes a human being and lives a mortal life, after which the divine form is resumed. One and the same god can thus be reborn any number of times. In Hinduism some gods, such as Vishnu, are thought to be regularly reborn as a human being, and sometimes even as an animal.

According to Christianity, one aspect of the divine became human in Jesus from Nazareth. This is said to have been a unique event with enormous ramifications, in that humankind was given the opportunity to be forgiven for their sins and to gain eternal life through Jesus.

Although Judaism and Islam generally hold the view that a human being cannot be a god, they both occasionally contain elements of the worship of "divine" individuals. For instance, Ali (the cousin of Muhammad) and other imams tend to be regarded as manifestations of the divine by some Shia Muslim groups. And in Judaism, in spite of its strict prohibition against the idea that a human being can be a god, the belief in the arrival of a messianic figure who will appear in conjunction with the coming to earth of the kingdom of God does leave some leeway for the notion of a "divine" human being. At intervals certain Jewish groups thus claim that the Messiah has arrived. The most recent outbreak of this longing for the coming of the Messiah was in New York as recently as the 1990s, among the Chabad Chassidic Jews. Generally speaking, however, neither Judaism nor Islam makes frequent claims to the divinity of the human being.

Individuals who have achieved the highest wisdom and insight and have thus become divine are another expression of the human god. The worship of such "godlike human beings" is particularly common in Eastern religions, but also occurs more or less openly in monotheistic religions. In Buddhism this is expressed in the bodhisattva ideal. A bodhisattva is an individual who has reached the deepest insights, but has chosen to return to earth time and again to help humanity to access the innermost truths and to shoulder the burden of human suffering.

In some religions, the highest religious leader is regarded as possessing divine qualities. The Egyptian worship of the pharaoh as divine and the Japanese imperial cult are examples of this phenomenon. (The latter was abolished dramatically when Japan was defeated during World War II, and the emperor himself declared the idea of the emperor as divine to be a "false myth.") In others, the souls or spirits of deceased forebears or holy men and women are worshiped and regarded as having developed powers after their deaths allowing them to affect the world of the living.

## A GOD WITH HUMAN QUALITIES

Sometimes the divine is seen as having human emotions and the ability to communicate with us directly, without being regarded as a human god. This aspect of the divine is common to many religions. The Greeks and Romans of antiquity, for example, believed in many gods who often represented human characteristics, such as fertility, fate, the warrior instinct, love, evil, good, and healing. The gods were often portrayed as behaving like human beings while also possessing supernatural powers. They were sometimes also ranked in a hierarchy of importance. In the religions of antiquity, the gods and goddesses were thought of as resembling human beings.

Similarly, Hinduism and Buddhism have gods and goddesses with human traits. They may be good or evil, and some of them have the same names and features in both religions. Both religions also speak of divine worlds. The individual gods may have limited powers and in this regard they bear some similarities with the angels of monotheistic religions.

Sometimes the gods are considered to be of human origin. That is to say, particularly successful human beings are transformed into gods. For example, the Chinese god of war, Kuan-ti, originated in a military commander who once lived on earth, and Imhotep was an Egyptian physician and architect (ca. 2600 BCE) who became a god after his death. Roman emperors were likewise sometimes worshiped as gods after their deaths.

Followers of monotheistic religions commonly regard their one God as having human features. The God of the five books of Moses is described as having many human characteristics, including the capacity for both wrath and charity, a desire to punish evildoers, the possession of a warlike or loving nature, and the ability to make demands. God has a voice and may even very occasionally be revealed to individuals. A chronological examination of the books of the Hebrew scriptures shows that the descriptions of God shift from a relatively accessible personality with human feelings in the early books to an increasingly distant God who is difficult to reach in the later ones. In the older scriptures God is in immediate, direct contact with humanity, but becomes more and more abstract and unattainable in the books written later.

According to Judaism, God stands in direct relationship to human beings. God's decisions may be affected by the prayers of people, as well as by human emotions and attitudes. And reciprocally, humankind has obligations to fulfill in relation to God. Some traditional schools of Islam also see the one God as having certain human feelings, although this tendency is less pronounced than in Judaism. In Christianity, when God is conceived of as "the Father" this aspect of the divine is often described in terms of human attributes, including charity, forgiveness, and love, but also punishment.

As a rule, a god with human features is also a gendered god. In monotheistic religions, God is often described in masculine terms. The divine as perceived in nature is often described as having feminine characteristics, one example being the term "Mother Earth." [1]

The god or goddess of fate is a form of god with human features governing the destiny of human beings that exists in some religions. In the Old Norse religions there are the gods Urd, Skuld, and Verdandi, for example, and there are Clotho, Lachesis, and Atropos in the religion of classical Greece. In other religions, such as Islam, this may be an aspect of the one God.

## THE CONCEALED GOD

*Go into your room and shut the door and pray to your Father who is in secret.*
—Matthew 6:6

Most religions, including those traditionally regarded as polytheistic, hold a belief in an ultimate being. Sometimes this God is comprehensible and fitted out with human qualities; at other times the highest God has no human traits at all, and is incomprehensible, indescribable, and concealed.

The hidden God who cannot be described may be experienced as more or less active in nature. In some schools of religion, this concealed God is regarded as the original creator who, having made heaven and earth, withdraws from the earth and lets it cope for itself. The task of this concealed God was to accomplish the creation and then merely to keep in existence the world we can experience. Sometimes the hidden God is not even responsible for the act of creation, which is carried out by some subordinate aspect of the divine. In other religions, God is given a more active role.

---

1. I have done my best to use inclusive language and have been careful not to assign a gender to the concealed God. Thus the words "he" and "him" have not been used in relation to the indescribable God.

In monotheistic religions, the idea of a concealed God is most evident in the mystical traditions. Inconceivable, indescribable, veiled, infinite, and free from human traits, the divine is in all things and thus also in human beings. Christian mystics may seek a God who is indescribable and inexplicable beyond the Trinity, Islam mystics may seek the aspect of the concealed God that is turned toward us and therefore accessible, and Jewish mystics may seek a God beyond the creator God of Genesis.

Even more traditional schools within these religions refer to a God who is beyond all similes and comparisons, including both those from nature and those from human characteristics. One example may be found in the Hebrew scriptures' story of Elijah:

Now there was a great wind, so strong that it was splitting mountains and breaking rocks in pieces before the LORD, but the LORD was not in the wind; and after the wind an earthquake, but the LORD was not in the earthquake; and after the earthquake a fire, but the LORD was not in the fire; and after the fire a sound of sheer silence. (1 Kings 19:11–12)

Another example is to be found in the Acts of the Apostles. Paul speaks to the Athenians, saying:

For as I went through the city and looked carefully at the objects of your worship, I found among them an altar with the inscription, "To an unknown god." What therefore you worship as unknown, this I proclaim to you. (Acts 17:23)

Eastern religions, too, refer to the concealed aspect of the Absolute, sometimes with other designations than the word "God." In Buddhism the deepest insights are not defined, because they cannot be described in words. Taoism (or Daoism) uses the mystical term "Tao" ("Dao") to designate the greatest power and the basis of all. Here, too, no attempt is made to describe the indescribable: "What is beyond this world the sages do not discuss, although they do not deny its existence" (Zhuang Zi, ca. 369–268 BCE). Hinduism contains the idea of a concealed divine primordial force, often designated Brahman.

In many religions, the highest, indescribable God is experienced as veiled but present in all creation. Thus, by definition, this concealed, indescribable God is close to one end of the spectrum of the notion of God: a pantheistic, all-embracing God who is to be found in nature.

## SOME CONCLUSIONS

Most religions allow for several conceptions of the divine. We thus find parallel descriptions of the divine as a more or less passive, impersonal, concealed force, the creator of the universe, an omniscient and all-powerful judge, a personal companion, or a divine human being.

In Hinduism this is a perfectly open process in which the gods are assigned different duties and roles. Other religions have sought other ways of integrating this diversity into a unity. The Taoist scripture *Tao Te Ching* offers the view that the highest truth may be expressed in many ways: "The nameless is the beginning of heaven and earth. The named is the mother of the ten thousand things."

In monotheism, with its basic belief that God is one, a great deal of effort is devoted to maintaining a unified image of God. This may be seen in the Christian theology of the Trinity, in which the divine is described as existing in three different manifestations while being fundamentally one. Such a God is concealed but also revealed to humankind, as in the burning bush, the pillar of cloud or fire in the desert, and the resurrection appearances of Jesus after the crucifixion.

This specific use of three forms of expression to describe the one divinity is also found in other religions. Buddha, for instance, is said to have three bodies. He may take on the emanation body in which he appears on earth in human guise, or the enjoyment body in which he appears in supernatural worlds, or the *dharma* body in which he has no human traits at all and is one with all buddhas and with the teaching itself. At the same time, these "bodies" are no more than different manifestations of one and the same reality. In Hinduism we find, correspondingly, the description of the three beings of God in the form of Brahma, Vishnu, and Bhagavan,[2] each of which represents some more or less concealed aspects of the single divinity.

---

2. Different schools of Buddhism and Hinduism use different names and designations.

In this way we human beings have sought to make the incomprehensible conceivable, in our attempts to entice the divinity concealed behind the veils to be revealed, so as to offer us a glimpse of the highest reality. And so the comprehensible aspects of the divine may bridge the gap, or be a form of communication leading us to the concealed God. We may also be unwilling to accept our intellectual and sensory inability to make all truths accessible for ourselves and so we create images of God our minds can embrace.

It is more difficult to grasp a God whose qualities are concealed, ineffable, and infinite than one described in terms of a father, a king, or a judge, complete with comprehensible human emotions such as anger and love—and many of the portal figures of religion were aware that this is so. Take, for example, this description of the way in which Jesus simplified his message to the people:

> With many such parables he spoke the word to them, as they were able to hear it; he did not speak to them except in parables, but he explained everything in private to his disciples. (Mark 4:33–34)

However, believing similes and symbols to be truths, as a Buddhist metaphor puts it, is "like a finger pointing at the moon and one must take care not to mistake the finger for the moon."

The great religious founders, deeply spiritual men with personal experiences of the divine, were well aware of this. The physicist Albert Einstein (1879–1955) put it very well: "The religious geniuses of all ages have been distinguished by this kind of religious feeling, which knows no dogma and no God conceived in man's image." However, the disciples and successors of the founders of religion did not always have the same spiritual experiences, with the consequence that sometimes the concealed aspect of the divine has had to make way for more readily accessible images.

One notion of God is described in strikingly similar ways in all the major religions: God as one, indescribable, infinite, and concealed. This is the image that appears to unite the systems of thought of the major religions with greatest consistency. Other aspects of God—the divine creator, the human god, the personal companion, the god in human guise, and so on—vary greatly from one religion to another and are thus beyond the scope of this work. They are certainly worthy of interest and attention, but my focus here is on that which unites rather than on that which separates.

Although there are discrepancies, too, in the ways in which religions describe the concealed God, the similarities are often surprisingly great. This is the main reason for which I have concentrated this volume on an analysis of the hypothesis that a concealed God does exist.

Few words have been given such varied content as "God," and few have been so abused. Furthermore, not all religions use the term "God" to describe the Absolute. However, with my Western background, I can find no other term to denote more satisfactorily that which actually cannot be named than the word "God."

## 〜 3

# Can There Be a Concealed God?

*No man can see God except he be blind.*
— Meister Eckhart (ca. 1260–1328)

WHEN WE CONSIDER the question of whether a concealed God exists, we must first examine our poten-
tial for obtaining knowledge about reality—and the limitations of these
capabilities. We human beings use our five senses to create an experience
of the world we live in. Let us assume that we wish to eat an apple. We look
at the apple, and see that it is red and round. We feel its smooth, rounded
surface. At the same time we take in its fragrant aroma. Then we bite into
the apple and hear that characteristic crunch. Finally, we experience the
taste. All five senses thus contribute to creating the concept of "apple" as
it is described and understood by most people. At the same time, it is
important to be aware that what one person may mean by the word "red,"
for example, may be different from another person's experience of that
color. Descriptions of colors and other sensory impressions are conven-
tions.

We may go on to make a mental experiment, attempting to describe an
apple to a person who was born blind, who only has access to four of the
senses. It seems perfectly possible, until we get to the description of the
color of the fruit. Suddenly there are no adequate words. In order to describe a color to someone who has no visual experience of color, we must
use abstractions that can only describe the sensory experience indirectly.

Now, what if no one had a sense of sight? Then in everyday language
we would have no words for colors. If someone happened to have an intuitive sense of the existence of colors, or had proved that colors exist
through a scientific experiment, it would still be impossible to explain
colors to others in a simple way, as language would not suffice.

The same holds true for each of our senses. It is impossible to describe concretely, to a person who was born deaf, what we experience when listening to music. A deaf person can feel the beat and the rhythm of music, but does not hear the tones and thus cannot have the whole experience. However lyrical our descriptions were, we could never capture the essence of music, or fully pass along the sensory impressions. What we end up with is circumlocutions and similes.

Let us make a second mental experiment. Imagine that, in the natural world, there were one hundred senses, but that human beings were only endowed with five of them. There is something to this idea, as we may see from the example of the bat, an animal that navigates using a sixth sense to register ultrasound. Bats can discover objects in the dark by emitting sound waves that bounce off the surroundings and then taking them in again on the rebound via a special sensory organ. We can never experience the sixth sense of the bat; all we can do is infer it.

Theoretically, then, if there were one hundred senses but human beings only had five, it would make perfect sense that there would be phenomena in the world we would be unable to perceive and grasp through our ordinary understanding. If God can only be experienced using senses we do not possess, we may only comprehend the divine through indirect explanations and emotional experiences. Furthermore, a person who has experienced God directly will be unable to describe that experience. Our language will not have the words for it, and circumlocutions or encouragement to try to experience the divine ourselves will have to suffice. Consequently, the answer to the question of whether God *can* be concealed in all that which has not been experienced has to be in the affirmative.

We may take the discussion one step further, using the color red as an example again. The experience of red comes into being in our consciousness as a consequence of light rays of certain wavelengths being reflected off a specific surface, such as an apple (though the experience of color does not come only from surfaces, as we can tell when we look at the sky). These reflected rays activate nerve cells in the eye. The impulses are conducted from there into the brain and "translated" to the perception of the color red. If there were no eye and no brain on our earth, the apple could not be perceived as red. In other words, without a beholder colors do not exist in the specific sense of that word.

We can reason in a similar way about other sensory impressions as well. For example, sound is a result of the ear mediating a specific oscillation to the brain. "The world around us" is thus a fundamentally subjective interpretation. We cannot imagine the "appearance" of a world that is not experienced by beings possessing consciousness. Taken to the extreme, we may say that living beings are a prerequisite for the world around us "existing" as it does.

## THE LIMITS OF OUR INTELLECT

Of all the species on earth, human beings have the most well developed ability to think. We have created written and spoken languages for the transfer of knowledge among us, for instance, making possible innumerable rapid developments in recent millennia in the areas of science, social organization, and culture.

At the same time, we cannot disregard the fact that the intellect we do possess is extremely limited in relation to how intelligent we could theoretically be. For instance, computers today can make their calculations millions of times faster than the human mind and are also that much better at storing information, although they are still emotionally and intellectually far less intelligent than a fly.

We might now consider the slightly naïve analogy that the relationship of the intelligence of a human being to a "greater intelligence" is about the same as that of a fly to a human being. Then imagine the fly buzzing into the ear of a fireman who is putting out a fire in Paris. The ability of the fly to understand that it is in the ear of a person whose job it is to extinguish fires in a country called France might be theoretically comparable to that of the human being to conceive, through the intellect, of the existence of God.

Perhaps the fly might unexpectedly have an emotional experience in the situation described above. Now imagine the fly trying, after extricating itself from the ear of the fireman, to describe this experience to its sibling. Even if flies have a language, its words would not suffice to describe that astonishing insight.

The philosopher Plato (ca. 427–347 BCE) described the limits of human experience using the metaphor of the cave. In Plato's cave, people sit bound, with their backs to the opening. Whatever happens there is reflected as shadows on the wall of the cave, and the people can only experience reality as portrayed two-dimensionally and in black-and-white. One day a man succeeds in escaping. He goes to the opening, looks out at the world, and is gripped by a sudden insight into how things "really look." Returning to his friends to describe what he has seen, he is faced with a problem. He has no words to make what he has seen real to his bound fellow human beings, nor do they possess any frame of reference through which to understand what they have not themselves experienced.

Correspondingly, we are bound by our intellect and our senses to a restricted experience of reality. There may be more spatial dimensions than the three we can experience, and certainly our "picture" of reality is limited and incomplete.

## OUR LACK OF PERSPECTIVE

A Taoist parable tells the story of a little fish who lived in the sea. One day he asked a larger fish what the sea actually was. "Everybody talks about it, but I can't see it. What is the sea?" The big fish explained that the sea was all around them and inside them. The sea brought them to life and when they died they would return to their origins in it. They were one with the sea.

The little fish cannot see the sea because he is in the midst of it and because it has always been there. This is also true of human beings' experience of reality. We are in the midst of everything and not having an overview of our situation, we are unable to see it as if from outside. At the same time, we live in a world we take for granted because we have always experienced it, and this contributes to further impairing our ability to see reality as it is. The fact that we do not have a larger frame of reference explains why it took until the seventeenth century for us to realize that the sun and the stars do not revolve around the earth, a discovery that was received with deep skepticism in its time. Similarly, insights regarding what reality "really" looks like may escape us because we do not have perspective on our situation. The human eye is another example. It can see "everything" except the eye itself. In that very way, we are in the midst of reality, with blind faith in our limited senses and our consciousness. We are like little fishes in an enormous sea.

## WHY IS IT SO DIFFICULT TO KNOW?

We rational beings of the twenty-first century are constantly flooded with sensory impressions at the same time that our intellects strain to solve each problem that arises and to remain in control of our complex lives. Thanks to all the material and scientific progress of the human race, we have firm confidence in our ability to use our intelligence to solve problems. At the same time, we believe more or less unequivocally in the experience of reality mediated to us by our senses. So what happens when we approach the thought of a concealed God from our usual angle?

This notion of God, whether or not it is real, is fundamentally an abstraction, beyond logic and proof. There is no getting around this fact, and therefore many religions share the theme that we cannot arrive at an experience of the divine via our five senses or our intelligence. The only feasible way of achieving this basically emotional experience of the divine is through our intuition. The rational, mentally hyperstimulated human being of today must therefore learn once again to return to the innermost core of being, in silence, to seek the answer to the question of God.

The search for God is no simple task, and as a rule it is a long one. Our spiritual experts describe the way in which layer after layer of sensory impressions and habitual thoughts have to be pared away before we can finally encounter an experience of the divine.

Sometimes, however, we are privy to the feeling that there is something more. When we listen to beautiful music or have an intensive experience of the fascinating natural world of which we are a part, we may suddenly experience a flash of insight into a reality that embraces far more than we can conceive of with our senses and our thoughts. The next instant it has vanished, and we wonder whether the experience was true.

At other time we may experience the dark sides of life opening up to us. Misfortune, betrayal, grief, or a feeling that there is no point in living may afflict us. We find we have lost our foothold and do not know who we are or what values to cling to. During such a period, we may be fortunate enough to feel life taking hold of us and gently moving us forward in a new direction. We may sense that there is a pattern and a structure to life that endows it with meaning, and that makes us feel graced. We may perceive ourselves as secure in relation to something larger than ourselves.

When the crisis has passed and we are back on *terra firma*, we may choose to believe that these feelings represented something true and real, or we may choose to interpret them as a series of coincidences, or an experience born out of the emotional chaos of the moment. It is on this knife-edge between truth and its opposite that every searching individual balances.

Why should it be so difficult? Why cannot God, if there is a God, be revealed once and for all, and thus put an end to all doubts? That is one way of asking. Another, the flip side, is to feel amazed that it is even possible to experience what is called "God" at all. Many people have wandered different paths throughout the course of history ultimately to reach a similar interior experience. From this point of view, we may feel that as human beings we have been endowed not only with senses and intelligence but also with a spiritual dimension that enables us to experience the divine. The concealed God is not utterly hidden. Just as we may find buried treasure, we may also find that which is buried in the very depths of "real" reality.

If the essence of God is concealed, we may ask ourselves why God was ever made known at all. Islamic tradition has it that God said: "I was a hidden treasure, and I longed to be known; so I created the world, in order to be known." The Jewish mystic Isaac Luria (1534–1572) held that God needs humankind, in fact, and is somehow incomplete without our seeking and our good deeds. The Christian mystic Meister Eckhart (ca. 1260–1327) was of the same opinion, and stated that God becomes aware of himself through humankind. Mystics of several religious schools thus assert that not only do human beings need God, the need is reciprocal.

We find that, theoretically, the preconditions for the existence of a concealed God are in place. But of course, theoretical possibilities are not always realized. Although many religions claim that God exists, there is no proof that they are correct. So how can we analyze the issue? One possible jumping off point is to investigate how the different religions describe that which is beyond our senses and our intellect, that which we, for want of a better term, refer to as "a concealed God."

## ᥱ Part II
# The Concealed God of Monotheism

THE RELIGIONS designated as monotheistic all originated in the teachings that developed in the area along the eastern shores of the Mediterranean. As the prefix "mono" plus the root "theism" imply, monotheism holds that there is only one God. All that is divine is rooted in this single, unifying power. Three religions are usually denoted as monotheistic: Judaism, Christianity, and Islam. There are other religions that also believe there is only one God, but in order to avoid confusion I use the term "monotheistic" here to refer to these three faiths alone.

The monotheistic religions all developed their own forms of mysticism, traditions that seek a God who is concealed and ineffable. Judaism calls its mystical tradition the Kabbalah, while Islam names its tradition Sufism. Although the mystical forms of the monotheistic religions have had some impact on one another, most of their developments have been independent.

None of these forms of mysticism exists in a vacuum, of course. Some of the books of the Kabbalah are used in traditional Judaism, and Sufism has had a deep influence on and may be seen as an inherent part of Islam. In the same way, Christian mysticism can hardly be delimited from the more ritualistic and traditional forms of Christian faith. Therefore, it is impossible to draw a clear line of demarcation between mysticism and other aspects of these religions. Moreover, the known history of mysticism encompasses many countries and epochs, spanning both the geographical spectrum and several millennia. These are important aspects to emphasize in any attempt to summarize some of the ideas of the monotheistic mystics concerning God.

## ~4

# God Is Not the Highest God:
# On Jewish Mysticism

JUDAISM HAS DEVELOPED gradually over a period of some four thousand years. Jewish tradition has it that Abraham founded the Hebrew nation when he converted his extended family to the monotheistic belief in one God. Then, some thirty-five hundred years ago, a course of historical events led the Jews to become slaves in Egypt. Some two centuries later Moses became the leader of a movement of liberation, and guided his people on the exodus from Egypt to Canaan, geographically situated roughly where Israel is today. Moses further developed Judaism, establishing a number of rites, laws, and norms. Later, the hub of religious practice centered around the temple in Jerusalem, which was destroyed in 586 BCE and rebuilt in 515 BCE.

As a consequence of a series of military defeats, the Jews were dispersed across the world. In about the year 70 BCE the second temple was also destroyed, and from then on the Jews were left to seek God by other means. This was the time of adoption of the laws and rites that still apply in traditional Judaism today. The mystical tradition or Kabbalah developed in parallel. When we consider Jewish mysticism in relation to more traditional Judaism, the following distinctions can be seen:

✦ Traditional Judaism emphasizes observance of the rules and laws found primarily in the Torah (the five books of Moses) and the Talmud (originally the "oral law" and its commentaries). Some of these laws are of a ritual nature, others are moral and ethical. Studying and observing the laws is a way of doing the will of God, and thus coming closer to the divine. Jewish mysticism also holds that these laws must be studied and observed, but emphasizes that there are other ways of seeking God. According to the Kabbalah, having basic knowledge of traditional Jewish literature is a prerequisite for commencing the mystical endeavor.

+ Jewish mysticism stresses the inner search for the divine. It is pursued using various spiritual disciplines and techniques, including prayer and meditation. Although prayer is an important aspect of traditional Judaism as well, it is not used for the inner search in a systematic way. In traditional Judaism, the search for God is more through study and the observance of laws and traditions, by which the divine may be experienced in everyday life.

+ Traditional Judaism has a tendency to interpret the religious legends and the statements attributed to God more literally than does the mystical tradition, where these descriptions are regarded more as symbolic.

+ In traditional Judaism, the importance of doing good deeds and complying with the laws is mainly for the sake of one's fellow human beings, while mysticism stresses the thought that God needs humankind in this regard.

+ Traditional Judaism is more centered on reason and logical thinking than is mysticism, where the focus is more on the emotional experience of the divine.

+ All schools of Judaism are fundamentally in agreement that we cannot ever completely comprehend who God is. In spite of this, traditional Judaism asserts the understandable and human qualities of God, while mysticism tends to regard God as altogether concealed.

In any effort to compare traditional Judaism and Jewish mysticism, it should be reemphasized that the line of demarcation between them is a blurry one.

## GOD AND CREATION

According to the Kabbalah, the Creator God of the Bible is not the "highest God." As opposed to the description of the deity in the Torah, the Kabbalah regards the highest, only God as completely veiled and ineffable. This may give the impression that the Kabbalah speaks of two gods, but that idea is inconceivable in Judaism. However, Jewish mysticism has a solution to this problem.

The concealed God, often referred to as En-Sof ("the infinite") is revealed in ten emanations (Sefirot). These bridge the gap between the real God and the universe we can experience with our senses. According to Jewish mysticism, the highest emanation of En-Sof functions as the God of Creation, the God described in Genesis. Thus the universe was created as a "function" arising from En-Sof, and in this way mysticism establishes the link between En-Sof and the God of the Torah as within the framework of monotheism. It should be borne in mind that this is one of the points of contention between traditional Judaism and Jewish mysticism. Isaac Luria, one of the central figures of Jewish mysticism, regarded En-Sof as having created the universe by contracting inward, a process referred to as *tsimtsum.*

Symbolically, Sefirot is described as having been intended to fit into ten vessels, six of which were, however, shattered at the time the universe was created.[3] After this accident, the shards of divine light and of the shattered vessels were spread throughout the universe. Had this not taken place, we would not have had to tolerate the incomplete world we live in today, with its evil, pain, and suffering. The aim of both God and humankind is to gather the shards and repair the broken vessels (the word for this is *tikkun,* meaning approximately "to repair").

The primary objective of humankind, according to Jewish mysticism, is therefore to restore the "divine order." This may be done mainly through good acts, observance of the laws, and drawing closer to God. Evil actions exacerbate the state of disorder, and the presence of God is said to be banished from the world. The more people there are who live righteously and seek the divine, the greater the chance that humanity will succeed in its endeavor. Every action of every human being is thus of significance.

An interesting position in Jewish mysticism is that God cannot accomplish this repair alone, but is dependent on humankind. "The impulse from below calls forth that from above," as the mystical scripture, the

---

3. In the myth about the vessels, Jewish mystical writers use symbolic language. Like practitioners of traditional forms of religions, religious mystics sometimes use symbols to elucidate the indescribable. In their descriptions, it is clear that they are aware that symbols are no more than deficient circumlocutions.

Zohar, has it. God is perpetually seeking humankind, but is not always able to reach us.

Why is it important that this aim be fulfilled? Jewish mysticism believes that our world was not the only world that was created. God has created and destroyed imperfect universes before ours. The thought that our world might meet the same fate is a worrying perspective that arises from these ideas. According to Jewish mysticism this makes it the responsibility of every human being to work for the perpetuation of our world, and to contribute to making it a better place to live in.

## WHAT IS HUMANKIND?

According to Judaism, God created man and woman, and after the fall, when Adam and Eve tasted the fruit from the tree of knowledge, God and humankind were separated, their natural contact disrupted. Every human being, however, retained a spark of the divine inside, and thus humanity has been left to seek a God who was henceforth concealed.

According to Jewish mysticism, the human soul consists of three intimately intertwined elements (referred to as *nefesh, ruach,* and *neshama*). As human beings develop, they are required to make use of the increasingly higher aspects of their souls. Nefesh is the lowest aspect of the soul, containing our instinctive behavior and our capacity to sin. Nefesh may also be referred to as "the animal soul." When a person begins to seek inner development, ruach, the next aspect, becomes important. This is the intellectual and moral side of the soul. This middle aspect represents the spiritual side of the human being, and in some respects functions as a link connecting nefesh with neshama.

Neshama is the highest aspect of the human soul, and is in direct contact with the divine. Although neshama is not conscious, it directs the "destiny" of each human being. According to some kabbalistic sources, this aspect of the soul may only be known after death. Other sources describe some very special human beings as having awareness of neshama during their lifetimes.

All three aspects of the soul exist before birth. When a person dies, two of them, nefesh and neshama, leave the body, while ruach remains for some time. Some sources hold that the nefesh aspect of the soul of a person who has committed evil may be relegated to the inferno for some time (usually no more than a year). Some scholars of the Kabbalah believe in a transmigration of souls, and that in the worst case the soul may end up in an animal, a plant, or even a stone. Other mystics reject the idea of transmigration. All human souls are said to be in mystical association with one another. Neshama, the divine aspect of the human soul, will be reunited with its source at death. The establishment of the kingdom of God will initiate the coming of the Messiah and the resurrection of those who have died, bringing the body and the three aspects of the soul into unity.

## WHAT IS GOD?

According to the Hebrew scriptures and its interpretations, God may have "human" feelings such as anger, sorrow, compassion, charity, regret, love, and the desire for revenge. Jewish mystics describe En-Sof as without these feelings, using terms such as "unreachable" and "indescribable." It is noteworthy that the concealed God, or En-Sof, is nowhere mentioned in the Hebrew scriptures or the Talmud. According to some Jewish mystics, God has neither the will nor the aim nor the plan that we would understand these terms. Neither does the concealed God intervene in or influence individuals' lives.

What then is God, according to Jewish mystics? Sometimes they describe the divine in terms of what it *is not*, since language does not have any way of expressing what it *is*. For instance:

+ God is not soul.
+ God is not body.
+ God is not intelligence.
+ God is not intellect.
+ God is not infinity.
+ God is not a king.
+ God is not mobility.
+ God is not stillness.
+ God is not spirit.

Jewish mysticism sometimes describes God as "nothing" (nothingness), meaning that the divine does not fall within any of the ordinary categories of human description. There are no words in any language on earth to describe who or what God is.

This means that those who have achieved contact with the divine face great problems. How can a feeling be described to those who have never felt it? The books we have read and the stories we have heard from people who have encountered the divine will not suffice for us to comprehend what God is. This is a problem with which Jewish mystics have long struggled, and their conclusion has often been that there is no choice but to be silent and allow every human being to pursue his or her own inner search for the divine. The paradox, not only for Jewish mystics,[4] is that the same people who assert that it is meaningless to try to describe God in words are also the ones who have written thick tomes about their mystical experiences.

## THE SEARCH FOR GOD

The last of the ten emanations, Schechinan (Malkut), is expressed in the reality we see around us. Everything, absolutely everything, is permeated by this radiance. Thus every human being has the spark of God within. This is what enables us to be aware of God's work. Unfortunately, God is not as readily accessible to our consciousness as the world around us. In order to achieve contact with the divine, a person must search, and this search can only take place inside the self.

The inward search may take place in many different ways, including various forms of prayer and meditation, all of which aim to silence the thoughts and impressions that normally besiege us. By doing so, we are able to penetrate the experiences of self and the world around us that disturb the experience of the ultimate reality.

This experience of the divine may be compared with our awareness of the stars in the sky. When the sun shines, its radiance dominates the world, and the stars—which are always shining in the sky—become invisible to the human eye. After sunset we may suddenly discover the other sources of light that have been concealed by the blinding rays of the sun. Similarly, the material reality we experience dominates our senses so entirely that the "sheen" from the divine is concealed. If we can slowly learn to close off (or penetrate) these sensory impressions, Jewish mysti-

4. For example, the Christian mystic Meister Eckhart often returns in his sermons to the question of what God is, although he also says: "And why do you prate of God? Whatever you say of God is untrue."

cism tells us that we will be able to discover the divine that has been there all along.

Prayer is a technique frequently used to accomplish this task, as prayer can serve as a form of meditation. The key to this form of prayer is not the words, but the intention of the person praying. One prays not with words but with the heart. This is referred to as *kavvana*. It is the feeling behind the prayer that determines its impact. Without feelings, prayer becomes meaningless. There is a Jewish legend of a man who had no prayer book and who therefore prayed using kavvana, simply pronouncing the letters of the Hebrew alphabet while turning his mind toward God. He said: "I give you the letters. I pray to you to form the right words out of them." The legend has it that this prayer went straight to God.

Some mystics stress the importance of a joyous approach to God. They see song and dance as a way of achieving a (sometimes ecstatic) experience of the divine. But here, too, the words of the songs, like the words of the prayers, are unimportant. The key lies in the emotion—the experience.

Some mystics have used the Hebrew alphabet as a "guide rail" for the inner search. Meditation on the letters is used as a way of focusing awareness on that which "is nothing and at the same time everything." The guide rail or banister gives the individual something to grasp in order to find the way and also serves as a guide for consciousness to find the way back to the "everyday" world when the meditation ends, so as not to become lost in the interior worlds. In medical terms this loss of foothold would be called a psychosis. Other religions, including Buddhism and Islam, also have their forms of meditation involving the chanting of letters.

One such meditation is on the name of God. The thoughts focus on the letters of the name that is so sacred it cannot even be pronounced. In Judaism, the full name of God is both sacred and secret. Knowledge of the name of God is said to give rise to tremendous forces that may be abused if they fall into the wrong hands. In the days of the temple only a few priests knew God's full name, and as time went on it was believed to have fallen into oblivion.

There are also meditations on the ten emanations of the Sefirot as a means of achieving an intuitive experience of the divine. This highest of them is Kether Elyon ("The Crown"), after which there are Hokhmah

("Wisdom") and Binah ("Understanding"). These latter emanations indicate that we may find the highest wisdom close to the divine essence.

According to the tradition, it is essential to approach the divine in a loving frame of mind. This love is meant to be love of both God and our fellow human beings. The significance of this message of love to Judaism is exemplified in the words of the Torah: "Thou shalt love thy neighbour as thyself" (Leviticus 19:18) and "Thou shalt love the Lord thy God with all thy heart, with all thy soul, and with all thy might" (Deuteronomy 6:5).

Nearness to God should be experienced in all aspects of everyday life. We are to do everything we do, from the trivial to the significant, even washing the dishes, with total concentration and presence. When one very well-known rabbi had died, one of his followers was asked what had been most important to the great master. The answer was, "Whatever he happened to be doing at that moment." Buddhism and Taoism contain similar thoughts.

Through the inner search we may arrive at different levels of perception and insight. Certain manifestations of God are to be found all around us every day, without our noticing them. They are part of the miracle of life. The search shows increasingly clear expressions of the existence of God before the divine is experienced directly. In this way, according to the Kabbalah, we can climb higher and higher, closer and closer to the highest divinity. In our thoughts, we may move through the worlds that separate the realm of the senses from the spheres of the indescribable, hidden God. Some Jewish mystics hold that we may achieve an ultimate perception of God, while others have it that we can only experience truer and truer manifestations of the divine, but never actually En-Sof. In this latter view, the divine may be compared with a tree, where the manifestations of God are the tangible, visible branches, while God is the root and the sap. The sap runs through the branches, but remains unseen.

At the same time, Judaism claims that every human being has the right, or even the obligation, to question everything, including God. This is an acknowledgment of the fact that the idea of a hidden, indescribable God cannot just be blindly accepted. Rather, we must seek, try to comprehend, investigate, and hopefully, finally find our answers to the great questions in life. According to Judaism, this is one of the main tasks for humankind.

Jewish mysticism stresses that the inward search for God must take place under the guidance of someone who has already treaded this path. Some of the methods that may be used can be hazardous if implemented in an uncontrolled way, as may be seen in the Jewish legend of four holy, wise men who made a mystical journey to the highest worlds. One died, one lost his mind, the third fell into idolatry, and only one, Rabbi Akiva, returned in peace to the world of the senses.

## 5

# *Beyond the Trinity:*
# *God in Christian Mysticism*

S OME TWO THOUSAND years ago, a man was born whose life and death gave rise to Christianity, the religion with the most practitioners in the world today. The history of the birth of Jesus has been documented in the New Testament, but we know very little about the life of this man before he stepped into the light of history at around the age of thirty.

The period Jesus spent preaching the gospel was relatively short: it is believed to have lasted no more than three years. During this time, it was clear from his message that he had deeply mystical experiences of the divine. Then he was arrested, crucified after a summary trial, and buried in a cave. Three days later, as Jesus himself had predicted, he returned, only to vanish once again shortly thereafter.

Jesus was well versed in the scriptures of Judaism, and his teachings are based on the Jewish religion, except that in some areas his interpretations were radical. Jesus himself stressed this link to the traditions when he warned his disciples, "Do not think that I have come to abolish the law or the prophets; I have come not to abolish but to fulfill" (Matthew 5:17), though he also taught that it was no longer necessary to observe the laws of the Sabbath or the dietary laws (see Mark 2:23–28 and 7:19). He attempted to make religion more accessible to the people by simplifying the message and disseminating it through readily understood parables:

> Jesus told the crowds all these things in parables; without a parable
> he told them nothing. This was to fulfill what had been spoken
> through the prophet: "I will open my mouth to speak in parables;

I will proclaim what has been hidden from the foundation
of the world." (Matthew 13:34–35; see also Matthew 13:10–17
and Mark 4:33–34)

The apostle Paul was the individual who found himself at the center of
developments and spreading the teachings of Christianity a few years after
the crucifixion of Jesus. Paul also described personal mystical experience
of the divine, writing, for instance, that he had been "caught up to the
third heaven" (2 Corinthians 12:2).

The revolutionary message in Christian doctrine is that Jesus was the
Messiah and that he was divine. It is clear that those who were close to him
gradually came to see him as the Messiah whose coming had been predicted in the Hebrew scriptures. According to the Gospels it is also probable that Jesus regarded himself as such toward the end of his life and
work: "Then he sternly ordered the disciples not to tell anyone that he
was the Messiah" (Matthew 16:20; see also Luke 24:44–47; John 4:25–26;
and John 17:3).

According to the Gospels, however, Jesus never stated directly that he
was God. It is not known to what extent Jesus regarded himself as being of
divine birth or as being "animated" by the divine, like other mystics. Some
time after his death, the view of Jesus as divine became generally accepted.[5]
After a battle within early Christianity (culminating with the Nicean synod
in 325) between the idea that Jesus had been born as God and the idea that
he was a high essence created by God, the belief that Jesus was born divine
and equivalent to the divine Father was accepted. This view has continued to prevail in the vast majority of Christian denominations.

After the crucifixion of Jesus, Christianity began to take a different
direction from Judaism. At about the same time Judaism ceased to proselytize, Christianity began to proclaim its message, becoming a religion
open to all. Although Christianity, like Judaism, is based on the Hebrew
scriptures, in Christianity the New Testament is regarded as having greater
authority. While Judaism is still waiting for the arrival of the Messiah,
Christianity asserts that the Messianic era began when Jesus, the son of
God, was born on earth.

5. The idea that Jesus was God may be discerned as early as the scriptures of the New
Testament, primarily John 1:18 and Romans 9:5. However, there is some controversy as to
the interpretation of these verses.

Like other religions, Christianity gradually split into many different forms. Christian mysticism reached its zenith during the first centuries after the death of Jesus, and flourished again in the early Middle Ages. There have, however, been great Christian mystics in later years as well, and the influence of mysticism is clear in contemporary Christianity.

## GOD AND HUMANKIND

According to Christianity, human beings were created in the image of God but were expelled from paradise after disobedience to God (the fall). The life of Jesus and his death on the cross, Christianity asserts, healed this wound to the relationship between God and humanity. Humankind was granted grace and eternal life.

In the Christian tradition the human soul comes into being at the same time as the body. The soul is personal and stands in direct relation to God. There are somewhat varying ideas about what happens to the human soul after death, but there are also basic ideas common to all forms of Christianity. If we have lived our lives in faith we will go to paradise, and live close to God. If a human being rejects God, for instance by committing evil, he or she may have to be purged in purgatory or in hell, far from the presence of God.

Many Christians hold that part of the human soul is divine. At the core of our souls we are bound to all of humankind and to God. This divine aspect of the soul is also referred to as the "spirit," and there is room for this divine Spirit to dwell in every human soul.

Christianity has no belief in reincarnation. This distinguishes it from the Eastern religions as well as from some forms of Judaism and Islam. To Christians, the life we live on earth is our only life, and is therefore our unique opportunity to find God and to behave righteously.

Christian monotheism is based on the concept of the Trinity, or the three aspects of God. These are separate entities, but always part of the same unity, and are traditionally referred to as the Father, the Son, and the Holy Spirit. As something of an oversimplification, we may say that the Father is the Creator God, the Son is the divine aspect that became flesh in Jesus and walked the earth, while the Holy Spirit is omnipresent and can be borne in all human beings.

The concept of the Trinity implies that some aspects of the divine are hidden, while others were revealed to humankind through Jesus. However, the concept of the Trinity is to some extent shrouded in mystery, and may therefore be seen as an expression of the inconceivable reality represented by the divine.

## GOD IN CHRISTIAN MYSTICISM

Some Christian mystics have spoken of another concept of God as well, a concealed God who is behind the Trinity and beyond that which can be described at all. Mystics known as Christian gnostics, who lived mainly in the first few centuries after the death of Christ, referred to the "divine essence." The gnostics held that the God we know from the Bible appears to us out of this divine source, but that the divine essence cannot actually be comprehended with humankind's limited capacity for understanding.

In Christian mysticism, too, there are attempts to put the indescribable into words. The divine experience may be portrayed in terms such as "light," "love," and "bliss," but only in full awareness that words can in no way suffice. Some mystics go so far as to claim that the Trinity of the Father, the Son, and the Holy Spirit have to be denied at some stage of human inner development if a person is to be able to experience the real nature of God. Any human being who achieves this insight also becomes divine.

Meister Eckhart, a German Dominican mystic, referred to the hidden God as the "silent ground" or the Godhead. Out of this silent ground arose the God of the Trinity. This description is reminiscent of the emanation from En-Sof out of which Jewish mysticism holds that the Creator God of the Bible appeared. Sometimes Eckhart goes so far as to say that the God of the Trinity exists *only* in the human psyche. This statement, like others of Eckhart, was not received well in all quarters. Eckhart was a controversial figure in Christianity at the end of his own life, and he has remained so.

The Godhead Eckhart discusses is beyond actual description and comprehension. There are neither words nor symbols to express this reality. Once again we see how mysticism—this time Christian mysticism—uses negations as a means of description. The divine is described, for example, as a non-person, non-reason, and even as "non-god." Once again, we see that the expression "nothing" is used to describe God, for instance by John of the Cross (1542–1591), the Carmelite monk who explained that the highest aspect of God does not exist, in the sense we normally attribute to the word "exist." According to Eckhart, the Godhead exists, but in a way that is beyond what we can experience, and God is thus separate from us: "When God created heaven and earth and all creatures, this affected His unmoved detachment just as little as if no creature had ever been created." This is a notion of God reminiscent of that used by the Jewish mystic Isaac Luria when he experienced God as so vague and difficult to reach as to have almost "contracted."

In this silent ground we discover the unity of all things: all is one. The entire universe is in every human being. From this it follows that Eckhart sees all aspects of the divine as being in the soul of every human being. We can find our way there through our search, just as the statue is already within the stone, just waiting to appear when the excessive material has been chiseled away. According to Meister Eckhart and some other monotheistic mystics, this is not a one-way relationship in which human beings come to insights about themselves through God, but rather a reciprocal one: at the same time, God comes to be self-aware through humankind.

As opposed to other religions, traditional Christianity holds that God appeared on earth at one time in the guise of a human being. Jesus was unique and the only savior. This belief is traced back to the words of Jesus himself : "No one knows the Son except the Father, and no one knows the Father except the Son and anyone to whom the Son chooses to reveal him" (Matthew 11:27); "No one comes to the Father except through me" (John 14:6).

However, there are Christian mystics who have a more complex view, such as Origen (ca. 185–254), who believed that the ultimate contact with God need not be mediated by Christ. In Origen's view, when the search culminates in unity with the divine, the seeker has become like the Son. Similar thoughts may be found in the work of Meister Eckhart: "Whatever he gave to the Son He intended for me and gave it to me just as much as to Him." Eckhart goes on to explain how we may all become the Son of God. He sees Jesus as filled with the divine in a way that may apply to any human being: "Whatever holy scripture says of Christ, all that is also true of every good and divine man." Interestingly, Jesus also expressed a similar idea when he quoted Psalm 82:6 during an argument with some of his fellow Jews in Jerusalem about whether he was committing blasphemy:

> Is it not written in your law, "I said, you are gods"? If those to whom the word of God came were called 'gods'... can you say that the one whom the Father has sanctified and sent into the world is blaspheming because I said, "I am God's Son"? (John 10:34–36)

The ultimate aim of the search is nearness to God. The opinions of the Christian mystics vary as to how close to the real God it is possible for a human being to come. Eckhart, Origen, the Syrian monk bar Sudaile, Thomas Aquinas (1225/6–1274), and the anonymous author of the book *The Cloud of Unknowing* all asserted that we may perceive an experience of total contact and unity with the divine. Eckhart went so far as to say that "God and I, we are one." Other mystics, such as Basil the Great, the fourth-century bishop of Caesarea, and the Flemish Augustine monk Ruysbroeck (1294–1381) speak of contact with the real God as something that can never be achieved. Basil asserts, for example, that we may only come into contact with the emanations of God.

This variety of experiences could reflect the "competence" of the different mystics for spiritual experience. Teresa of Avila (1515–1582) was a mystic who described her encounter with divine reality as a journey through an interior castle with seven stories and many rooms. Moving from one to the next, a person may experience higher and higher intimations of the divine. The anonymous author of the mystical work *The Golden Fountain* describes an inner journey similarly, as leading to closer and closer contact with the divine until the seeker is finally united with and becomes one with God. This notion bears resemblance to Paul's view expressed in his first letter to the Corinthians: "But anyone united to the Lord becomes one spirit with him" (6:17).

One of the key themes of both traditional Christianity and Christian mysticism is love. The divine is seen as *pure love,* as the source out of which human love is born. Human love is not only the love we feel for our neighbors and for God, but also for all of humanity and for everything that lives. Humankind must endeavor to give as much love as possible in both words and deeds. The highest form of love is given unselfishly, putting the prosperity of others before our own.

The words of Jesus instructing people to "love your enemies and pray for those who persecute you" (Matthew 5:44) highlight the centrality of this idea to Christianity. Someone once asked Hillel, one of the great interpreters of Judaism, to define Judaism while this other person was standing on one leg. Hillel replied, "What is hateful to you, do not do to your neighbor: that is the whole Torah; all the rest of it is commentary." Jesus took this message of love one step further, altering the command to show consideration for our fellow human beings to a command to do good deeds: "In everything do to others as you would have them do to you; for this is the law and the prophets" (Matthew 7:12).[6] According to Christianity, it is this unselfish love that will be the salvation of the world.

## THE SEARCH FOR GOD

According to some translations of the Gospels, Jesus told his disciples that "the kingdom of God is within you" (Luke 17:21). Christian mystics believe that the interior search is the means of coming into contact with and experiencing the divine. While Eastern religions often use the term "meditation" to describe this inner search, Christian mystics sometimes use words like "prayer" and "contemplation" for such methods.

Prayer may take different forms. One would be contemplation upon the complex, paradoxical notion of the Trinity, the aim of which is to illuminate the fundamental incomprehensibility and ineffability of the divine. Prayer may also be directed toward Jesus or toward a sacred individual such as the Virgin Mary, or a saint. Particular verses of prayers or lines from the scriptures may be recited over and over, and are thus reminiscent of the mantras of Eastern mysticism.

Another technique, also found in the search for God in other religions, is concentration on breathing. To focus on one's breathing is to concentrate one's awareness on a single point. In Christianity, this type of breathing exercise is often done in conjunction with the repetition of a formulaic prayer originating in the Eastern church and known as the Jesus Prayer: "Lord Jesus Christ, Son of God, have mercy upon me."

Some Christian mystics regard abandoning the ego, the personality, as

6. See also the early Christian document the *Didache* (1:2), dating from approximately the year 100, and according to which Jesus makes a pronouncement similar to Hillel's negation.

a prerequisite for contact with the divine and thus as a part of the inner search. Paul expressed this thought when he wrote to the Galatians that "it is no longer I who live, but it is Christ who lives in me" (2:20). A central theme in Christian mysticism is that every human being should strive to become as much like Jesus, the ideal human, as possible, and Jesus likewise stressed the importance of having an attitude marked by humility when he told his followers, "Whoever wants to be first must be last of all and servant of all" (Mark 9:35; see also Matthew 18:3–4 and Luke 10:21). Jesus and several of his followers held that self-denial and the renunciation of what appear to be the sources of pleasure in this life paved the way for the highest insights and eternal life:

> For those who want to save their life will lose it, and those who lose their life for my sake will find it. For what will it profit them if they gain the whole world but forfeit their life? (Matthew 16:25–26)

We should cease clinging to our material possessions. Like spiritual seekers in other religions, Christian mystics also sometimes retreat into solitude. Jesus and his predecessor John the Baptist sometimes withdrew into the solitude of the desert (see Matthew 4:1–2, Luke 1:80, Luke 5:16, and Matthew 14:13). When we are alone, we are no longer bombarded by sensory impressions and it becomes easier to focus our thoughts. Christian convents and monasteries have provided a tranquil environment for prayer and contemplation, and were sometimes, in fact, established in sheer protest against the increasingly worldly shape religion appeared to be taking.

All these forms of meditation and prayer aim to concentrate awareness so that silence can be achieved. In a peaceful, quiet frame of mind, a human being can experience the divine—not with words and images, not even through sensory impressions or thought. In the words of the gospel according to John, "No one has ever seen God" (1:18). The experience of God is unique and indescribable. It can never be mediated, only perceived.

Christian mysticism has sometimes portrayed the mystical way as having three stages: purification, enlightenment, and, finally, unity (with the divine). One thought that occurs regularly in the works of Christian mystics is that although a human being may prepare him- or herself for the encounter with God, the real, ultimate experience of the divine can only be mediated by God. Jesus also said of the ability of humankind to enter the kingdom of God: "For mortals it is impossible, but not for God; for God all things are possible" (Mark 10:27). A Christian seeker may progress through prayer, meditation, and a true spiritual attitude, but in the end it is the grace of God, through Christ, that bears human beings forward to unity with the divine.

## ～ 6

# Behind the Veils:
# God in the Mysticism of Islam

ISLAM WAS FOUNDED in western Arabia by the prophet
Muhammad (ca. 570–632). After a series of visions in
which Muhammad heard and saw the archangel Gabriel, he began to
preach the new teachings. Islam has many points of contact with Judaism
and Christianity, and practitioners of Islam pray to the same monotheistic God, whom they call Allah. The most important book of Islam is the
Qur'an, where the visions and teachings of Muhammad were recorded. In
Islam, both Moses and Jesus are regarded as holy men and prophets.
According to Islam, the Arab people, like the Jews, are descended from
Abraham, whose sons Ishmael and Isaac were the forefathers of the Arabs
and the Jews, respectively.

As different schools of thought developed within Islam, Sufism took its
place as the Muslim form of mysticism. Sufism and more traditional Islam
are intimately intertwined. Traditional Islam stresses the importance of
living in observance of laws and traditions as the central theme even while
recognizing the importance of the inner search for God. Sufism gives this
inner search for the divine a higher priority, emphasizing the search for
knowledge through personal inner experience yet still valuing the observance of the law. One must stand on a solid ground of traditional knowledge before the true inner search can begin.

Some Islamic mystics have been strongly influenced by traditional religion, and they describe their notion of God through the use of human
and comprehensible attributes. The idea of God as ineffable and indescribable that dominates Sufism is also important in traditional Islam.

The question of the extent to which God is separate from the world and humankind is a central issue in Islam. In one view, Allah is described as superior to and distinct from the creation, including human beings. The essence of God is "beyond us." A person may only hope to come *close* to God, through studies of the Qur'an, for example, where the divine may be discerned in the text. In this view, it is not possible for an individual to achieve "communion" with God.

Others hold that God exists in the creation, and thus in every human being. The search for God implies an inner quest through which a person may find and be united with the divine, which exists in the deepest recesses of the human soul. In its explicit form, this view is not unlike pantheism, and may even result in human beings perceiving themselves, in moments of mystical union with the divine, as "being" God.

Traditional Islam tends to assert that God and humankind are separate. Sufism, however, has diverse views on the subject of whether the innermost depths of human beings are divine. The belief that a human being may find and be united with God in the depths of the human soul is, however, held by many Sufi, and is the view that will be the main focus of discussion in the remainder of this chapter.

## GOD, THE CREATION, AND HUMANKIND

Like the other monotheistic religions, Islam holds that the world and its inhabitants were created by the one God. Before the creation, God entered into a pact with all unborn souls and the destiny of human beings was thereby sealed. People are seen as being born to this world to learn about the creation, and after death as traveling back to God, the source.

The soul exists before birth, and after death the soul is once again separated from the body. The soul awaits judgment day, when the world will be destroyed and then recreated by God. On that day the soul will be reunited with the body. The evil are relegated to inferno, the good go to paradise.

In Islam, it is clearly stated that if humankind does not follow the intention underpinning the creation, the result will be misery and the eventual destruction of our world. This thought may also be found in Jewish mysticism.

## WHAT IS GOD?

*Since you cannot speak in words about the essence of God, best of all speak about nobody at all.*

—Kitab-Ilahi

According to Sufism, God can only be described in metaphorical, symbolic language. Thus Allah is described, for example, as "the first cause," "a buried treasure," "the light," and "the only true reality." The divine is everywhere and everything in the universe, including all living things, are at one with God, who is perfection. This insight cannot be attained with our external senses or our intellect; rather, it may only "become visible through the heart." The term "unity," an experience of God's transparency in all things, may be used to describe what many mystics find when they reach the goal. The divine is also timeless and eternal.

In this experience of the divine, a human being may become one with the universe. The Muslim mystic Abd al-Qadir al-Jilani (1077–1166) held that a person is separated from God through the illusion that there is anything that exists apart from God. All is God, but in everyday life we tend to be unable to discover this unity, because our own concentration is far too fragmented. (Hinduism describes the all-embracing principle of the divine, Brahman, in similar terms. Sikhism, with its roots in India, refers to a God who contains many of the elements to be found in both Islam and Hinduism.)

Sufis are aware that metaphors and symbols cannot possibly reveal the divine. All attempts to make the notion of God visible only lead us further from the truth: "To be a Sufi is to detach from fixed ideas and from preconceptions." Silence is regarded as the most successful way of relating to the concealed God.

Love is a theme that runs throughout Islamic mysticism, particularly the love of God. Love originates in God and flows through humankind— but this is not just any kind of love. The emotional experience we most readily come to think of when we hear the word "love" is only a pale shadow of the supernatural, pure, unselfish love that flows through human beings when they encounter the divine. The longing for the highest divine love is one of the *leitmotifs* of Sufism. If God exists in all beings, love may be directed toward all living things. Sufism holds that a human being in real contact with the divine will always meet others lovingly and unselfishly.

Some Sufi assert that what we may experience as divine cannot truly be God but only the attributes of God, and that the real God will always remain hidden. Our limited intellects can only reveal to us God's work, and give us an intuitive experience of the side of God that is turned toward our world, symbolically referred to as "the face of God."

Other Sufi sources say that a seeker may reach unity with the divine, sometimes described as a union of love. A few mystics, the most prominent of whom was al-Hallaj (ca. 855–922), went so far as to state "I am the Truth," which in fact means "I am God" since " Truth" is one of the names of God. To say the least, others found this statement off-putting. Still other mystics see the mystical union as taking place within the divine aspect of a human being. It has been said that through humankind God can be revealed to God.

## THE SEARCH FOR GOD

There is a parable explaining the importance to the Sufi of nearness to God. In the days when there were as yet no bodies but only souls, the souls were lined up and the world was displayed to them in a vision. Most of the souls ran toward the vision. After this, the remaining souls were shown paradise, and most of them rushed toward this vision. Those who were left were shown hell, and nearly all of them turned and ran away. After this, a divine voice was heard asking the remaining souls who had not permitted themselves to be influenced by any of these visions what it was they actually wanted. And the souls answered, unanimously, that all they wanted was to be close to God.

True knowledge of God comes only from personal experience, and a Sufi is willing to make great sacrifices in order to have such experience. If God is in each of us, a human being may experience the divine by turning inward. The key is more in the experience of the divine than in faith or intellectual conclusions.

Sufism holds that insight into the insignificance of worldly things is a vital step along the way toward God. Material possessions are therefore to be renounced. Giving up money, property, and objects may be prerequisites for coming into contact with the divine. However, for a Sufi, forgoing one's earthly possessions is not enough in itself. Another central theme of Islamic mysticism is that we must abandon our "selves" if we are to be united with the divine (a process referred to as *fana*). We must renounce all feelings of prestige, pride, accomplishment, fear, and hate that make up our personality. The self has to be sacrificed if we are to attain the insight that all individuals are united with one another and with God. This is how we subordinate ourselves to the divine.

To an outsider, renunciation of the self may appear to be a great sacrifice. For those who have wandered this path toward "the universal self," however, and who have left the ego and worldly assets behind, there is no doubt that far more is gained than lost. It is said that the inner world that is achieved gives total satisfaction and makes the personal endeavors of the outside world both unnecessary and uninteresting.

The search for the divine may be described as a journey into the interior of the human being. Muslim mysticism sometimes speaks of "the seven essential spiritual stations" we may journey past to reach God. This is the emotional and ethical ideal that should be sought in the successive search for the divine. Those who walk this path must fully master each level before moving on to the next. The inner search may be facilitated by periods of living in seclusion. Briefly, the seven essential spiritual stations are:

1. *Repentance.* In this first stage, there is a change, a transformation in the life of the individual that results in the taking of the first steps along the way of the search for the divine. This awakening is generally preceded by a life crisis. At this stage the person becomes aware of all the evil committed, and in the process of atoning for these sins a decision is made never to commit evil again.

2. *Temperance.* The aim of this kind of restraint is to cease doing what is forbidden. Religious and societal rules must not be violated, and "the voice of the conscience" must be obeyed. Abstention from earthly pleasures is also included here. This stage is meant to awaken fear (of God) as well as incipient hope.

3. *Renunciation.* At this stage interest in worldly things and earthly honor and fame fades. The individual's former values and priorities change, and the desires to achieve previously held aims are lost. Self-obsession is left behind.

4. *Poverty.* At this level, the journey toward inner knowledge becomes

tangible, and economic value loses all importance. The less the individual carries along, the lighter the journey. The person learns to abstain from material possessions and from the desire for material welfare.

5. *Patience.* Patience enables a person to handle both physical and spiritual pain, and gives him or her the strength to deal with human weaknesses and flaws. Patience is also a tool for learning to manage conflicts and hostility. Mastering this level leads to inner maturity, tolerance, and wisdom.

6. *Trust in God.* At this stage the individual achieves knowledge of and complete confidence in God. The unity of all things and of the kinship with all life is experienced. At this stage the individual is prepared to surrender entirely to God.

7. *Contentment.* At the seventh and final station, total inner satisfaction is attained. The individual becomes "whole": a joyful, loving, and wise person. This also means complete acceptance of the world as it is and an experience of full communion with all aspects of nature. This state is never-ending.

The Sufi methods that may be used for coming into contact with the divine are many and varied, with different forms of meditation as the central theme. Many of the techniques are similar to those used to find God in other religions. Initially, the aim of the exercises is to close out external sensory impressions and to quiet one's thoughts. Slowly, attention comes to be focused inward. Sufism also stresses that the actual point is not to find God, but to recollect the divine. It is returning to that which has always been.

Tradition has it that Allah has ninety-nine names. Each one has a different meaning, and each has its occasions for use. Recitation of these names is used in some techniques of meditation. It is said that "God has ninety-nine names; one who counts them will enter paradise."

Another technique is to chant the attributes of God. As in all the monotheistic religions, short prayers may be repeated time after time in order to help shut out all "everyday" thoughts and to focus awareness. Sufism also uses techniques reminiscent of those used in Eastern religions, including breathing exercises similar to those of yoga.

Song and dance may also be used to bring the seeker into the kind of ecstatic state that may result in a sense of contact with the divine. One example is the whirling dervishes, who dance faster and faster as they strive to still all their inner thoughts. The aim of such dancing is the dissolution of the individual personality and the achievement of unity with the only true reality. This, too, is a form of meditation.

Islam, like Judaism, has many rules and laws. These are central to Sufism, where they are seen as a means of attaining perpetual awareness of God (known as *dhikr*). A person wishing to live in constant awareness of God must also have the right attitude to everyday life. In this respect, the prophet Muhammad serves as the highest ideal. A life lived morally and virtuously is a prerequisite for the highest insights. Sufism also sees the laws and the scriptures as having a "hidden" meaning that can be learned from a wise spiritual leader and can provide extraordinary, deep insights.

According to Sufism, in order to seek the divine one must have a teacher who has achieved inner knowledge of God. This teacher or *pir* must have both intellectual and spiritual knowledge, in which case the pir will be able to lead others to these higher insights. Traveling this road alone is considered ill-advised, difficult, and even dangerous, and as being associated with the risks of both madness and evil. A Sufi mystic, Ibn al-Arabi (1165–1240), noted that "he who has no master will find that Satan is his master."

But none of us can ever travel the way fully of our own accord. No matter how much we renounce, suffer, and struggle to achieve the divine we will only be able to reach a certain point at which, paradoxically, we must abandon the journey. Only divine intervention can bring us to the goal of our spiritual travels. This intervention is nothing we can strive to call forth; it will simply come to the individual who is ready to receive it and who has waited long and patiently. In the end, the seeker is at the mercy of the eternal God.

## ✎ Part III
## The Concealed God in Eastern Religions

---

THE WORDS "EASTERN RELIGIONS" are used here as an umbrella term for Hinduism, Buddhism, Taoism, Confucianism, Shintoism, Sikhism, Jainism, and other religions which, as a rule, developed in Asia out of one another or from ancient systems of belief. Hinduism, for example, grew up thousands of years ago out of the Vedic religions. Hinduism, in turn, was the breeding ground for Buddhism. As they have developed, these religions have also influenced one another, some more and some less. Many Eastern religions have a firm focus on the individual search for the highest truths. Thus aspects of what the monotheistic religions often regard as mysticism are central elements in many Eastern religions. The following chapters offer a brief description of the ideas of the Absolute as they are put forward in four Eastern religions: Hinduism, Buddhism, Taoism, and Confucianism.

## ✌ 7

# *God and Gods in Hinduism*

A S OPPOSED to other major religions, Hinduism has no
known founder, nor can we date its establishment.
This is partly because Hinduism developed over a long period of time,
and partly because Hinduism could, in fact, be described as a number of
religions, in that its many practitioners hold highly variable views. The
fact that Hinduism has managed to retain the designation of a single religion can be attributed to the tolerance and freedom of thought Hinduism
displays, both within its own beliefs and practices and in relation to other
religions. This diversity also makes it difficult to summarize the ideas of
the divine in all the schools of Hindu thought. The focus below is on the
form known as the Vedânta.

## THE UNIVERSE, LIFE, AND DEATH

According to Hinduism, the universe had no beginning. There was no
creation arising out of nothingness, nor will there be an end: "The universe, or nature, is without beginning or end. There was no time when
nature did not exist." There have always been and will always be worlds.
Therefore, the reality we experience is nothing but one of an infinite number of worlds. Worlds are constantly being created and destroyed, and
there are parallel worlds that are not aware of one another.

Hindu mythology has both creator gods and destroyer gods. One frequent theme is that Brahma creates worlds, Vishnu preserves them, and
Shiva eventually destroys them. Some schools hold that all this is accomplished at the orders of a higher god, sometimes referred to as Krishna and

sometimes as Bhagavan, the primordial god. At the same time, the various gods are fundamentally aspects of one and the same "quintessential being."

Our world is populated by numerous souls. They are eternal and cannot be destroyed. Some time after the death of a human being the soul is reincarnated and returns to the world in the body of a new individual. During periods when the world is destroyed and before a new world has been created, the souls sleep a dreamless sleep. Plants, animals, and human beings all have souls, as do gods, demons, spirits, and other beings of which we are not usually aware.

During the course of a human life, every human being collects karma, in direct relation to deeds. Good deeds bring positive karma, while evil deeds accumulate negative karma. Karma determines rebirth, to either a higher or a lower being. A life lived as a good and insightful person will thus mean reincarnation into the body of an individual of higher standing, while a life lived in evil and unawareness will lead to rebirth as a person of lower standing or occasionally even as an animal. This is the way in which Hinduism expresses the existence of a moral world order.

Ultimately, if a person should succeed in abolishing all the negative karma, there would be no rebirth. Rather, after death, that person would become one with the mystical concept of *moksha* (corresponding to the *nirvana* of Buddhism). To our Western minds, it may appear that it would be undesirable or unwelcome to achieve moksha. Why would we endeavor and struggle with the aim of vanishing altogether from life on earth? But Hinduism holds that it is only our limited insight that makes us cling to the thought of wanting to live our worldly life forever and ever. Attaining moksha is regarded as the most desirable state. Some schools of thought have it that it is possible for a human being to proceed to this ultimate destination by dint of personal effort alone, while according to others divine grace is the only way for a human being to take the final step toward salvation.

## GOD IN HINDUISM

At first glance, Hinduism appears to be full of gods. There are gods of creation, gods of destruction, gods of happiness and of death, of thunder, fire, wind, water, and sun, just to mention a few. There are also gods who have wandered the earth in the form of human beings to teach the truth. These gods include Krishna, Rama, Vasishta, and Manu.

All these gods may be seen as an expression of the human need to "costume" the divine. It is easier for many people to seek something with attributes and an appearance than to try to find a God whose only designations are "nothingness," "indescribable," or "concealed." The monotheistic religions and Buddhism offer fewer opportunities to fit out the divine with various qualities. The primary dogma of monotheism is that there can only be one single God, and Buddha's original idea was for every human being to carry out a personal search, without the assistance of any god. In Hinduism, the idea of a multiplicity of different gods has always been accepted, and the result is that there has always been access to a number of "guises" for the divine. The many gods of Hinduism are often seen as manifestations of the one God, and thus are means of perceiving this God, whose essence it is so difficult to capture and define.

One example of the way in which Hinduism expresses the link between a diversity of gods and the idea that they are essentially one may be found in the *Bhagavadgita*. The eleventh song portrays a conversation between Prince Arjuna, who is of two minds as he prepares to go into battle, and his driver, who turns out to be an incarnation of the god Krishna. In order for Arjuna to perceive the true Krishna, he is given divine eyes. Arjuna says, in astonishment and with great respect:

My dear Lord Krishna, I see assembled in Your body all the demigods and various other living entities. I see Brahma sitting on the lotus flower, as well as Lord Shiva and all the sages and divine serpents.

Who, then, is the "highest" god in Hinduism? The answer comprises a variety of characteristics and names, depending upon whom we ask. There are five designations of the divine that have special positions: Krishna, Vishnu, Shiva, Bhagavan, and Brahman. Brahma is a god with personal attributes, while Brahman denotes a divine soul of the universe, or a principle. Brahman is regarded by many as being the basis and prerequisite for all things.

Others regard Krishna as the highest god. Some Hindi claim that there are many Brahmas, one for every world, and that they are all subordinate to Krishna. By legend, Krishna has also been incarnated in a human form as recently as a few thousand years ago. Thus Hinduism manages to equip god with the highest, hidden power while it also describes the same god as having amused himself on earth.

Vishnu is a god of Hinduism whose status has risen over time. Some forms hold that Krishna is an incarnation of Vishnu, the one who "preserves the world." Vishnu is also the god Hinduism predicts will return to earth in an incarnation by the name of Kalkin, who will establish an era of happiness on earth. Thus Hinduism is one of the many religions with a messianic idea. Other Hindu believers claim that Shiva is the god who is the true ruler of the universe.

This diversity of gods may be seen as irreconcilable with the idea of monotheism. However, the Hindu believer sees it simply as a way of trying to describe a reality that is beyond all words and that stands above all contradictions. In this real reality there is perfect unity, and thus only one God, irrespective of name. The Rig-Veda declares that: "Existence (or Reality) is One, though the wise ones call It by various epithets."

The personal attributes assigned to the divine are sometimes regarded as attempts by human beings who have not yet achieved enlightenment to describe the ineffable. Various stages of spiritual development are outlined, the first being one in which human beings conceive of God as having personal qualities and as the creator of the universe. In the next phase, God is seen as a universal, active force contained within every human being. At the highest stage, a person realizes that God, the soul, and the universe are one and the same. When a person attains the highest truth, it is no longer necessary to refer to the divine as having human attributes or, as the Upanishads put it:

It is not understood by those who (say they) understand It.
It is understood by those who (say they) understand It not.

The divine is everywhere. This may also be expressed by saying that God is everything; thus, the divine may be found in every living being. In Hinduism this eternal core in each human being is referred to as "Atman." Atman is associated with (and at the same time actually is) Brahman, the soul of the universe that may be found everywhere in creation. Every human being is divine, and at the same time connected to every other human being and everything in the surrounding world. This human core can never die. The *Bhagavadgita* describes the human soul in these words: "It was not born; It will never die: nor once having been, can it ever cease to be."

Becoming aware of Atman means attaining the highest insight, the greatest knowledge of all. Just as a poor man may live for many years in a hovel with a buried treasure under the floor and have no idea that he is wealthy, many of us live our lives completely ignorant that we bear Atman, the greatest treasure, inside ourselves.

The concealed God in Hinduism, as in the mystical traditions of all religions, has no tangible properties or qualities. God is indescribable, but at the same time God is the foundation or basis of everything. The highest (and only) Hindu God is said to set the world in motion and keep it spinning, while at the same time being a totally immovable and immutable God.

God is also described in opposites. For example, it is said that God is immutable, and also faster than the spirit, that God is nameless and also has thousands of names, that God is distant and at the same time very, very close. Negations (God is *not* this, that, or the other) are also used to describe the indescribable. Once again, contradictions and paradoxes are used to bring to human beings the insight that God is a force, an existence that cannot possibly be compared with the things we experience through our senses and in our minds. We may only approach God inside ourselves, in silence.

In Hinduism there are divergent opinions as to whether God is responsible for the laws of karma and of nature that hold in our world, or whether these laws stand above the divine. Buddhism tends toward this latter interpretation.

*Lila* is a special concept in Hinduism meaning "the play of God," implying that God actually had no real motivation in creating the world, but created it simply as a source of diversion, a kind of plaything. The idea is not unique to Hinduism. Plato, for one, said that "man ... is made to be the plaything of God, and this, truly considered, is the best of him." The idea of human beings as the playthings of God is also found in Jewish mysticism. Taoism, too, has its similar statements about the idea of the world order at play in nature.

The idea that everything around us—and many other phenomena as well—were created solely as the caprice of a playful divinity may feel like a bit of a comedown to an individual whose life has been devoted to seeking meaning in creation. Still, the idea of a God at play may allow us to refrain from fruitless theorizing about something that is and will remain concealed. "Giving up" on that which is fundamentally incomprehensible may thus, in fact, open the way to attaining the highest wisdom.

## THE SEARCH FOR GOD

It has been said that "in Hinduism realization of God is the whole of religion." Achieving an inner experience of and contact with the divine is thus the cornerstone of Hinduism.

In Hinduism, most people are considered as living in "illusory reality" or *maya*. Although we try to enjoy life, we are often unable to see the whole picture, and find ourselves enmeshed in detail. We live in a world of names and shapes, and learn that the world is constructed of different parts and that spirituality and matter are separate. We experience our "selves," our personalities, in this external reality and we see the world as revolving with ourselves as the center of the world. We relate to the world around us and divide it into "I," "you," and "it."

But according to Hinduism, this is not "true" reality. In reality, everything is *one*, a single unit. Maya is no more than a pale shadow of true reality, although it is sufficient to attract our attention, and thus to entice us and exacerbate the inner search for the divine. Maya clothes us in layer upon layer of psychological coverings, the thickest of which is the outermost one, the body. Thus our experience is encapsulated into this "I."

The self is the main obstacle along the way to "participating in the divine life," to moksha. As all we can see is our self and the illusions of our external world, we believe that the highest meaning in life is to fulfill our material wishes, satisfy our desires, and search for the pleasures of life. This is the creation of karma that attaches to our soul and, in turn, leads us into the eternal cycle of reincarnation.

We might counter that since there is so much that is good about life, there are benefits to the idea of rebirth. And it is true that in the many lives of the soul, the individual may experience some happiness and well-being. But according to Hinduism, life and, ultimately, death bring this pleasure to an end. In fact it is brief and transitory. The only way to attain assurance of eternal salvation is to break the eternal circle of birth and death and become one with moksha. Only through contact with the divine can we achieve the necessary wisdom and insight to be able to cease clinging to passion and desire and to become good, loving individuals, which is the way to salvation. The Upanishads say: "He who knows that highest Brahman, becomes even Brahman."[7]

There are many ways of attaining direct contact with the divine, according to Hinduism. As Hinduism developed in a geographical area that may be likened to an enormous experimental laboratory with a very high level of tolerance for seekers of all kinds, it is natural that it should be open to a wide variety of spiritual disciplines and techniques. All ways that lead to insight about God and to wisdom are regarded as good, including many different forms of meditation, with their various methods of breathing, mantras (individually adapted words or phrases) to focus the mind, prayer, and a variety of bodily movements.

To begin with, the individual must be released from all the needs associated with the self, and then eventually from the very self. We must cease to seek earthly pleasure and abstain from hate and from behaving badly toward our fellow human beings.

*Bhakti* is a key term in Hinduism, meaning single-minded devotion, surrendering to unselfish love, and celebration of God. "He [God] is the Essence of love." This enables us to receive the ultimate insight, or enlightenment, that comes to the individual who is ready, through grace. The seeker then finds that love, the lover, and the beloved are one.

Yoga is, in some ways, a contrast to bhakti. Yoga is about attempting to control both body and soul. Breathing is at the core of yoga methods, which include control of other bodily functions as well, and efforts to quiet the flow of thoughts and reach a state in which the senses are at peace so that contact with the divine may be achieved.

There is a beautiful Hindu metaphor in which our consciousness is likened to a lake where waves ripple the surface. As long as the waves are there, the surface is not transparent. Not until we can bring our consciousness to stillness, bring the waves down, can we look down into the depths, where we discover the divine inside ourselves.

---

7. Similar statements may be found in other religions. However, the medieval Jewish philosopher Yehuda Ha-Levi's statement, "If I understood Him, I would be Him," should probably be interpreted to mean that it is fundamentally impossible to comprehend God.

What happens when an individual attains moksha? Attempts have been made to answer this question, describing how we become one with the soul of the universe of which we have always been a part, although we have not known it. Other descriptions include the cessation of all longing for selfish pleasure. But, as always, we are forced to admit that words cannot suffice to describe the indescribable.

Simultaneously, we note that in Hinduism not *all* souls are expected to be redeemed and become one with moksha. There will be no ultimate salvation for the world. Instead, the universe will go on existing, as it always has, with new worlds being constantly born and old worlds dying, and with our souls revolving in the eternal cycle.

## ◦ 8

# Buddhism: A Religion Without God?

S OME TWENTY-FIVE HUNDRED years ago, a man left his family, his wealth, and his position behind in search of the highest knowledge. He had been born a prince and was brought up in an overprotected environment where he never needed to consider the dark sides of life. When, as an adult, he was confronted with human suffering for the first time, with aging, illness, and death, this man, Siddhartha Gautama, was so traumatized he decided to abandon everything to seek the truth.

He began by seeking a master to help and guide him. He was in contact with many of the wise men who lived and worked in India at the time, but he failed to find the guidance he sought, so Siddhartha Gautama determined that he would have to pursue the search on his own. Over the years he subjected himself to long periods of fasting and other types of mortification, in combination with various kinds of meditation and yoga. After six years of great privation, he realized that bodily suffering was not his way to insight, and he turned elsewhere.

Legend has it that Siddhartha Gautama sat down under a banyan tree for the meditation that would lead him to full insight, known in Buddhism as "enlightenment." He attained this highest state the very first night, and found the great truths. Thus Siddhartha Gautama became Buddha, the "Enlightened One."[8]

After continuing his meditation for forty-nine days, Buddha decided to

8. According to Buddhist tradition, Siddhartha Gautama is one of a number of Buddhas. Here, the name "Buddha" refers to him unless otherwise specified.

return to the world and pass down what he had learned. He followed this vocation until his death, at about the age of eighty. He communicated his learning to a large number of disciples, who in turn passed his wisdom and insights along to others.

Buddha made three claims that differentiated him from the majority of other Indian religious practitioners at the time:

+ that the many gods were subordinated to a highest truth, an eternal law;
+ that a life in mortification of the flesh, an ascetic life, was not the best path to knowledge;
+ that every human being, irrespective of cast, race, and previous learning, could attain the highest truths.

Since the death of Buddha, his teachings (dharma) have been passed down from generation to generation. Buddha did not attempt to found a religion with fixed structures and regulations, rites, and traditions. To him, the important thing was the way. The way could lead an individual to the same insights Buddha himself had attained. Thus his teachings did not appeal to others to believe in a dogma or a given faith, so much as to accept a method for working one's way to the highest knowledge. The core of Buddha's teachings includes the "four noble truths":

+ the truth of suffering;
+ the truth of the origins of suffering;
+ the truth of the cessation of suffering;
+ the method that leads to the cessation of suffering.

Buddhism, like other religions, eventually split into various forms, differentiated in terms of beliefs, traditions, and norms, but still containing a set of central Buddhist themes.


## THE INDIVIDUAL, LIFE, AND DEATH

The main theme of Buddhism is the inner search for truth. While some religions have come to emphasize external rites, traditions, and customs more and more, Buddhism has retained its central teaching, that each individual must seek insight in his or her own consciousness.

The knowledge being sought is no less than the deepest insights about everything. Our restricted senses only allow us to experience fragments of truth about the world, but as we have nothing else to relate to, these over-simplifications appear to be all of "reality." A meditative inner search may lead us to insights as to the real structure of the world.

Our sensory impressions and our thoughts pose major obstacles to experiencing the true reality because sensory impressions constantly create the images and experiences we are taught from earliest childhood to interpret and believe in. They provide us with the information we need for survival, and with security because we share them with others. They can be communicated since we have a language for them, and we can thus tell others what we see, hear, feel, smell, and taste. At the same time, we are constantly being bombarded with sensory impressions, which means that our consciousness is never at peace. Furthermore, our consciousness has a steady maelstrom of thoughts and feelings running through it. We think in words, in images, in sounds, and in feelings. Our consciousness is constantly full of thoughts and without practice we cannot possibly still their flow for even a moment. And yet, according to Buddhism, a still consciousness is a prerequisite for coming to see reality as it actually is.

According to Buddhism, it is impossible to attain a full understanding of the structure of our world through our sensory impressions, philosophical ruminations, or the use of scientific methods. Reality can only be comprehended by moving beyond sensory impressions and thoughts, allowing insight to be awakened within us. Total knowledge is always within us, but we cannot awaken it until we are able to ignore the perpetual "din." The reality we then find cannot be described in words.

Neither does Buddhism see total understanding of how the universe, life, and death function as the only aim. When we reach the highest insight, we are unified with the incomprehensible, known in Buddhism as nirvana. What makes this so important is described below.

Reincarnation is a central thesis of Buddhism (as in Hinduism, but with different views of what parts of our "consciousness" are carried over into the next life). According to Buddhism, we may be reborn as new individuals, but even in different "realms," one of which is the realm of humankind, where we are at present. What body we are reborn into will depend on the karma we have accumulated in our previous lives. Our karma consists of the acts—evil, neutral, and good—we plan and carry out. The negative karma we collect may just as well result in our being afflicted by suffering in this life as in the next. Similarly, good deeds may result in a positive development of this life or the next. Thus the universe is governed by the law of cause and effect, a kind of "moral law of nature." In this respect, Buddhism is like the other major religions of the world, among which there is consensus as to the existence of a higher spiritual significance to the performance of good deeds.

Why do we commit evil or good acts, and thus accumulate karma? Buddhism holds that we do so because we cling to material things and transient sensory experiences. We collect wealth and possessions. We work hard to climb the career ladder. We seek pleasure through sensual experiences. Sometimes we know happiness, but it is often brief. One of the central themes of Buddhism is, therefore, *dhukka,* the idea that life is full of suffering. Dhukka has a second meaning as well, which is disappointment over the transience of the superficial pleasures in life. The world is in a constant state of flux. Material things and all life are continually changing and being reformed.

The aspects of Buddhism that deal with suffering have sometimes been interpreted in the Western world as being a sort of pessimistic, life-denying philosophy. However, Buddhism has a different angle on the matter of suffering in life. Suffering enables us to grow and develop. Life, with its suffering, challenges us to seek that which is right—to collect positive karma and to reach higher and higher insights. Positive karma and insights lead, in turn, to higher and higher forms of life and ultimately to becoming one with the Absolute, nirvana. An understanding of suffering and of the way to the cessation of suffering is a prerequisite for this development.

There is one other obstacle to becoming one with nirvana, and that is our personality, the idea that every individual is unique. Like other religions, Buddhism asserts that we have to renounce the experience of the "self" in order to attain the highest insights. This way of reasoning is based on the principle of the variability of all things. If every aspect of every human being is no more than a little building block in a state of constant change, what then is a personality? Buddhism answers this question by concluding that the "self" does not actually exist, but rather the notion that we are unique impedes the highest insights.

The ultimate unity with nirvana breaks the spiral of birth, suffering, and death. As will be seen below, that which happens in nirvana is beyond all words but, according to Buddhism, there is no question that it is a state far superior to the life we live here on earth.

## GOD IN BUDDHISM?

Buddhism is sometimes referred to as an atheistic religion, a religion without god(s). Although some forms of Buddhism do their utmost to avoid the word "god," it does appear, along with similar terms in various contexts:

*The gods that surround us.* The original form of Buddhism had a multiplicity of gods. Buddha himself refers on various occasions to different gods who were important at the time in India. The night he struggled to achieve enlightenment, for example, he was embroiled with the evil god Mara, who fought against him. It is probable that Buddha used the designation "gods" to symbolize, describe, and explain human feelings that might otherwise be difficult to understand.

*Divine worlds.* Buddha describes different worlds, one of which is inhabited by human beings and another by the gods (his own mother was reborn into this world after her death). What makes Buddha's teachings about gods so original is that he describes their power and significance as limited, and they themselves as subordinate to a higher truth. In this way, becoming one with nirvana is moving to a level higher than that of the gods. Not even the gods can reach nirvana without being reborn as human beings along the way.

*Buddhas and other enlightened individuals.* Although Buddha himself opposed the idea of worshiping a person, in some forms of Buddhism a cult has arisen around the idea of Buddha. This cult idolizes not only the Buddha who walked the earth under the name of Siddhartha Gautama, but also other buddhas it believes existed. Some schools of Buddhism worship and pray to other enlightened men as well, who are said to be able to help us not only in this life but also after death. For instance, the Buddha of the Infinite Light (Amitabha) and the founder of Tibetan Buddhism, Padmasambhava, are prayed to. It should, however, be emphasized that it is not the human beings Siddhartha Gautama or Padmasambhava who are prayed to, but the symbols or ideals they represent as spiritual men. Worshiping enlightened men is not unlike the Christian worship of Jesus, except that Christianity has gone one step further in claiming that Jesus was born divine.

Thus the idea of gods can be found in Buddhism, but the question of what the term "god" refers to remains to be answered. As a rule Buddhists turn against the idea that when they speak of "gods" they are referring to the understanding of God that monotheism and Hinduism hold, with their belief that God (or gods) have created and maintain the universe. Ultimately, then, Buddhist teachings appear to imply that gods and divine worlds are to be regarded as mental constructs that may be used to aid us in our search for the highest truths, but to reach enlightenment it will be necessary, eventually, to abandon these notions. Here we may recall the words of Christian mystic Meister Eckhart: "I pray God to rid me of God."

How do Buddhist teachings then compare with the idea of a concealed, indescribable God as we find it in the mystical traditions of monotheism and in Hinduism? Let us recall before embarking on such a discussion that the mystics of monotheistic religions have asked whether there is any point in our using the term "God" in our attempts to approach this concealed reality. What we seek is something completely different from all human notions, including our ideas about God. Buddhism shares this attitude, and states that the highest reality is not "God."

Buddhism uses the term "nirvana" to describe the state in which all ties with the world have been cut. Buddha had four areas about which he refused to provide any explanations, asserting that it was not meaningful to do so, that these truths could not be made comprehensible with the words of ordinary language. For this reason, we cannot know what knowledge Buddha had of these areas, one of which was nirvana (the others being the relationship between body and soul, the origins of the universe and of life, and the limits of the universe in time and space). Thus Buddha spared himself answering the question of what this highest reality actually is.

Although nirvana cannot be conceived of or described, Buddha's teachings indicate the following:

+ *Nothingness.* Nirvana, the highest reality, is described as "emptiness" or "nothingness." However, this does not mean the kind of emptiness or nothingness we imagine using our limited intellects, but something entirely different that our language does not have the words to describe. *Sunyata* is a term with roughly this meaning.

+ *Unity.* Sometimes Buddhists describe the universe as a unit, in which *everything* is interrelated. Thus every human being is both a part of this unity and at the same time an entire cosmos.

+ *Negations.* Like the monotheistic mystics and Hindus who, for want of words, describe God in terms of "not," Buddha, too, used negations to describe nirvana: "There is that sphere where there is neither earth, nor water, nor fire, nor wind; neither sphere of the infinitude of space, nor sphere of the infinitude of consciousness, nor sphere of nothingness, nor sphere of neither perception nor non-perception; neither this world, nor the next world, nor sun, nor moon. And there, I say, there is neither coming, nor going, nor stasis; neither passing away nor arising: without stance, without foundation, without support [mental object]. This, just this, is the end of stress."

+ The Absolute is described as a "cosmic awareness," of which our individual consciousnesses are a part. Most of us are ignorant of this fact, but when an individual attains the higher levels of insight it becomes evident.

+ According to Buddhist tradition, we all have nirvana inside ourselves, whether we know it or not. This aspect of ourselves is called "nirvana element" or "Buddha nature," and may be likened to the Atman of Hinduism or the belief of the mystics of monotheism that we all bear the divine inside ourselves. Nirvana has also been described as a state of consciousness.

+ The law of karma is intimately intertwined with the way to nirvana. The deeds we do during our brief lives determine whether or not we will approach the Absolute.

And so, until we decide to seek the truth, we remain puzzled about the real meaning of the words "nirvana" and "Buddha nature." In this respect, the teachings of Buddha differ from many other religions. Because Buddha does not define absolute reality, there is no need to oversimplify, distort, or be dogmatic—needs that have forced many religions into crusades against other religions, as well as into internal disputes and apostasies. Instead, Buddha put all his concentration into pointing out a way in which the individual could pursue his or her search, the only path to insight. Because Buddha preferred not to speak out on the subject, we cannot be certain as to whether nirvana is equivalent to the concealed, indescribable God of Hinduism and the monotheistic mystical traditions. We may simply conclude that this may, perhaps, be the case.[9]

## SEEKING THE TRUTH

As in the monotheistic mystical traditions, in Buddhism the inward search is the only way by which we can experience the highest truths. The methods vary from one form of Buddhism to the next, but certain principles apply throughout.

One step on the way to the highest knowledge is the practice of meditation. The initial aim of meditation is to neutralize the thoughts that constantly occupy our minds by focusing on one single phenomenon, such as our breathing, an image, or a mantra. Another is to meditate on an "unanswerable" question, such as "What did your face look like before you were born?" or a paradox like "What is the sound of one hand clapping?" Total concentration of awareness on a single point may bring the churning of our minds to a standstill. Alternately, we can learn not to react to the constant stream of thoughts, but to simply note and observe them, and then disregard them. It is a major undertaking to learn to both concentrate and relax sufficiently to be able to neutralize our persistent thoughts. Once this has been achieved, at first for brief instants and later for longer periods of time, we learn to use the focus of our awareness to pursue the inward search.

In the next step, a meditation may focus on suffering, concentrating our thoughts on the transience of life, its pain, death, and rebirth. Another theme for meditation is the law of cause and effect. The meditation should lead us to a feeling of compassion for and empathy with all life.

According to Buddhism, all things are in constant flux, and this ephemerality also applies to our own bodies and our minds. For this reason, some exercises in meditation aim to experience the constant changes in one's own body and mind. This teaches us that the "self," each individ-

9. The question can also be reversed, so we ask ourselves whether some mystics in monotheistic religions may have found what Buddhism refers to as nirvana.

ual's personality, does not actually exist. The experience of non-self is one of the cornerstones of the search in Buddhism, and a prerequisite for the highest insights.

Living life in the right way is the basis of the human endeavor to reach the highest levels of insight. Good deeds, empathy with all living things, humility, and compassion for others are qualities that lead to wisdom and pave the way toward enlightenment. Meditation alone is not enough, because a life marred by evil deeds will always block the path to spiritual development. This means that the greatest service we can do for ourselves is to learn to live for others, as expressed by the fourteenth Dalai Lama:

Foolish, selfish people are always thinking of themselves and the result is negative. Wise selfish people think of others, help others as much as they can and the result is that they too receive benefit.

Through meditation, contemplation, and righteous living, human beings pass to higher and higher levels of insight. Sometimes this development is slow and gradual, but progress may also be rapid. Some forms of Buddhism hold that enlightenment may be attained in this life, others that there is a window of opportunity for a short period after death when it is possible to become one with nirvana. If we prepare thoroughly for this moment during our lives, then we may reach the highest level of existence when the time comes. Thus death is portrayed as a unique opportunity.

Buddhism places great responsibility with the individual. The inner search can only be initiated and carried out by the person him- or herself. At the same time and like other major religions, Buddhism stresses that we need a master in our search for knowledge, a guide who is well versed in the techniques of meditation and the innermost truths.

## ~ 9

# Chinese Religions:
# God in Taoism and Confucianism

BOTH TAOISM and Confucianism originated in China. Although there are vast differences between them, their common roots are to be found in a traditional Chinese explanatory model applying to the reality beyond sensory experience. According to this way of thinking, the human being, the microcosm, reflects a reality beyond the senses, the macrocosm.[10] The world, including the laws of nature, are seen as controlled by cosmic phenomena, some of which are fundamentally outside human comprehension.

The primordial forces of the universe, yin and yang, are opposites that also balance one another. It is this balance that keeps the universe in harmony. Yin and yang represent negative and positive, female and male, passive and active, and other contrasting pairs. Yin and yang represent opposites, but at the same time there is always a component of the one in the other—each thing also contains its antithesis. Darkness is never completely black; we can always find a trace of light. No human being can be entirely evil, or entirely good.

In addition to the existence of a hidden world order governed by specific forces of nature, this original religion also had a number of both gods and demons. Another aspect of this tradition was the worship of deceased ancestors. As a rule, these personal expressions of the divine are overshadowed by "the concealed world order." One of the most important

10. Similar thoughts about the macrocosm and the microcosm may be found in the writings of Plato, in Hindu thought, and in the works of monotheistic mystics.

tasks for humankind is to try to understand the forces and laws that govern the world, including their flow, so that we may fit into the harmony of the universe.


## TAOISM

The man who is regarded as the founder of Taoism, Lao Tze, is a figure shrouded in myth. Legend has it that the wise Lao Tze was so disappointed in his fellow men that he decided to leave the country. A border guard pleaded with him not to leave until he had committed his insights to paper, and so Lao Tze wrote the *Tao Te Ching*, the basic scripture of Taoism, and then crossed the frontier, never to be heard of again.

What is known as Philosophical Taoism is a mystical religion in the deepest sense of that concept. The original formulators of Taoism had the good sense not to simplify things, putting symbols forward as truths. Instead, they fully accepted the fact that some aspects of reality are beyond the limited capacity of our senses and that descriptions and circumlocutions can never reveal the truth. The term "Tao" cannot actually be defined or described, but it is often translated as "the way," highlighting the Taoist idea that we should be provided with methods rather than force-fed dogmas. Tao also represents the concealed pattern, of which nature may make us aware. At the same time, it stands for the innermost truths and the highest principle. Tao is everywhere and has always existed because it is beyond time, but Tao is also formless and completely hidden. Tao is the greatest force out of which everything arose. At the same time, Tao is described as emptiness and as the darkness out of which the light arises. Tao is absolute, exists in every thing, and is simultaneously immutable.

The highest truths are therefore not subject to description, but can only be experienced inside oneself. Our five senses can never reveal Tao, which is very different from the things that can be defined in the world of the senses:

> Look, it cannot be seen—it is beyond form.
> Look, it cannot be heard —it is beyond sound.
> Grasp, it cannot be held—it is beyond intangible.

This Absolute should not be given a designation or a name, according to Taoism, because words do not suffice and will only inhibit our minds. Therefore Taoism, too, uses negations to describe the indescribable. However, the highest ideal is silence, since no words can possibly describe Tao: "He who knows (the Tao) does not (care to) speak (about it); he who is (ever ready to) speak about it does not know it."

The term "god" is not used about the highest truths in Taoism: it would be far too restrictive. Tao has no human traits, unlike gods, who are often described in terms of personal attributes. Although some Taoists worship gods, most deny the significance of personal gods and a belief in a god as creator of the world. A term that does often occur is "the mother," as an attempt to describe the primordial force symbolically.

Tao may be sought by turning inward, through contemplation and meditation. Such practices release the consciousness from disruptive thoughts and impressions and create space for Tao. The way of the interior voyage is not through theoretical knowledge or intellectual thought, which can actually keep us from experiencing the mystery that is Tao. According to Taoism, the words of our languages only lead to fragmentation and categorization of reality. They alienate us from unity, which is true insight. It is in the interstices between thoughts and words that we can find the highest truths, or perhaps more an intuitive sense of how reality is structured. There is no point in wondering what the right questions are, nor is it meaningful to seek the right answers. Instead, we must learn to "think without thoughts" and to allow our intuition to be our main guide in this wordless search.

Taoists point out that we are accustomed to fragmenting reality into its component parts in order to analyze, define, and describe it. What that also does, however, is to deprive us of our sense of the whole. In a holistic experience we can attain true understanding of how all things are interrelated and function together, and we can gain emotional insight into Tao.

Life is to be lived in joy—a natural pleasure that comes from within as a result of living in accordance with Tao. Instead of disturbing the balance of the universe with our egocentrism or our evil, we must strive to subordinate ourselves to the eternal law and to live in harmony with it. This makes Taoism a way of life, a way of achieving harmony with the universe.

Nature is very important to the view of this balance in Taoism; human beings are meant to live in harmony with the natural world. If we live in concord with all else, we will do that which is true and right. But we must never use our abilities to serve our own egotistical purposes. The moment we act in line with our selfish needs, the way forward will vanish for us, shrouded in mist.

Taoism believes we should strive for passivity of a kind that will result in activity because it allows the concealed forces of existence to work through us. The Taoist word for this non-activity is *wu wei*. Instead of attempting to control, endeavor, and struggle, we should learn to be like the water, to "flow" with the current of existence. All we need to do is to make ourselves available as a tool for the greatest of all forces. Thinking and being should become one. But to practice wu-wei we must also learn to give in, to abandon control.

Further, we have to renounce even the search to find the true way: to realize in all humility how little we know is the way to open ourselves up to the great insights. To do this, we also have to dare to let go of our accustomed ways of viewing the world.

The idea is not that we should sink into introverted contemplation. Tao cannot be understood, it has to be "lived," and it is in everyday life that we may encounter the great truths. Everything is experienced as a whole, and in this experience the insight that the "self" is nothing but an illusion may come to us. According to Taoism, a world in which everyone strives to open up and to live in accordance with Tao will be a world that flourishes. In this way, Taoism is more than merely an individual way of life; it is at one and the same time also the way of society and of the universe. Living in accordance with Tao also leads to a sense of belonging, of oneness with all things. The line of demarcation between the individual and the surrounding world is effaced. Thus the enlightened individual may meet life and death with exalted tranquility because they are basically one and the same. When life comes to an end the body dies, but not the eternal Tao: "Whoever dies but maintains his spiritual power has eternal life."

As individuals come to live more and more in Tao, they eventually develop a kind of goodness that radiates from within, rather than being attached from the outside in the form of ethical and moral norms. Evil deeds harm not only the individual but are also injurious to the harmony of the universe. All individuals are of equal significance, according to Taoism, and each of us has a special function to fulfill.

A person who lives in Tao achieves the highest wisdom. This wisdom comes from within, and cannot be attributed either to intelligence or to analytical ability, only to living in harmony with the highest truths. By abandoning oneself to Tao, a person opens up to and can be guided by inner wisdom. Then external actions will come of their own volition, rather than being planned or prepared for.

## CONFUCIANISM

Confucius (551–479 BCE) developed a combination of religion and philosophy based on humanism, morals, and ethics. In his view, human beings are good by nature, but ignorance may trigger evil. Confucius shouldered the task of opening the world to an understanding of this knowledge. Human beings should be "worthy, open-hearted, truthful, zealous, and good." Like the representatives of other religions, he used the expression "What you do not wish for yourself, do not impose on others." The relationships of human beings to one another are central to the ethics of Confucianism, in which respect for the family has high priority. While Taoism stresses the importance of the inward-turning search for the true world order and for harmony, Confucianism is considerably more focused on giving practical advice and instructions for how life should be lived.

The teachings of Confucius refer to the existence of a cosmic order, Tao, stating that we should never be separate from Tao, not even for a moment. Taoism and Confucianism often use the same terms, but sometimes with different senses. The word "Tao" as used in Confucianism may be used to designate the righteous "way" of the individual. Like Taoism, Confucianism does not provide exact definitions of this word, so although "Tao" does not appear to be as mystical a term in Confucianism as in Taoism, there is still room for interpretation.

One of the central missions of humankind is to emulate the cosmic order here on earth. We may do so by living a life ensconced in rituals and ceremonies, but also by having respect for the world around us and for our forebears. In combination with a morally righteous way of life, rituals are the best way to approach the human ideal state. However, it is not sufficient for us to observe the external forms. To achieve completion, our external actions must be directly linked to a righteous inner attitude and frame of mind. This state of balance between outward actions and inward mood does not appear out of nowhere, but can be achieved over time as a result of righteous living. In this sense Confucianism and Taoism agree that the ideal human being is one whose actions are always complete and are always spontaneous in the present.

According to Confucius, the purpose and end of living righteous lives is not only the transformation of the individual, who becomes a better, more harmonious person by living in accordance with moral and ethical principles, but also the transformation of humankind. If more people choose to live in accordance with basic ethical values, the entire world may eventually become a moral paradise. This makes *all* human lives significant. As opposed to some other religions, Confucianism sees the future paradise as arising not in any other world or dimension, but on our very own earth.

The effacing of the ego experience that is so central to many mystical forms of religion is not significant in Confucianism. Instead, the emphasis is on the fact that we *are* our social relations. Without them we are nothing, and every individual is an important part of the human community.

Confucius did not refer to a personal god who governed good and evil, although he did not exclude the possibility that spirits existed.[11] Neither did he state that goodness leads to personal gain in a life after this. Rather, Confucius said these matters were too difficult to be understood by him and so he refrained from speculation about them: "While you do not know life, how can you know about death?"

Confucius did refer to a highest truth he designated as "Heaven,"[12] which can be interpreted as "destiny" or "world order." According to Confucius, there is a basic moral law inherent in the world order, and it influences the course of history. The wise human feels "sacred veneration" for the will of Heaven. Confucius claimed Heaven had sent him to accomplish

11. It may seem paradoxical that people began to worship Confucius and to idolize him as a god several hundred years after his death.

12. In Judaism, the term "Heaven" (Ha-Shamayim) is sometimes used to refer to the divine. See, for example, Daniel 4:25 in the Masoretic text "that the heavens do rule" (which, in the NRSV, is translated as "the Most High has sovereignty").

his mission, but that appears to be as far as he went in speaking about what is beyond the world of the senses. One of his contemporaries said of him: "His discourses about man's nature, and the way of Heaven, cannot be heard."

Later practitioners of Confucianism have gone on to develop the idea of Heaven. Chou-Tse (1017–1074) designated this principle as "nothingness," because it is beyond comprehension, and Shu-Xi (1130–1200) spoke of Heaven as a force governed by unique rules.

## COMMON ROOTS

Taoism and Confucianism developed out of common roots, though over time Taoism became a religion of the mystical, intuitive search and Confucianism a religion based on the rational and the practical. While Taoism holds that intellectual knowledge cannot provide ultimate insight, Confucianism sets great store by book learning. Confucianism was built up around rules and principles, while Taoism developed into a religion strikingly free from dogma. In some ways they are opposites, and yet many practitioners live with one foot in each religion. The truly wise person is not disturbed by the inherent paradoxes, but instead regards them as important steps toward insight.

In spite of their differences, the line of demarcation between Taoism and Confucianism is a blurry one, and the two religions share a core of beliefs, including the idea that the universe is governed by hidden forces that are fundamentally beyond human comprehension. It is not far-fetched to compare this idea with similar thoughts about the ultimate reality described in other religions as a concealed God, but this possibility can neither be confirmed nor denied.

# ᴖ *Part IV*
# Science and God

*The cosmic religious experience is the strongest and noblest driving force behind scientific research.*
—Albert Einstein

THE CREATION MYTHS of the major religions came into being thousands of years ago. Like ourselves, the human beings who inhabited the earth then had to find ways of dealing with the mysteries of life. Their minds were preoccupied with questions about when and how the world was created, where human beings came from, and what are the boundaries of the universe. Since the means for conducting scientific studies were severely limited, our forebears depended on their intuition and imaginations, and these were the sources of the myths on the origins of the world and the reasons for our existence.

Not until the seventeenth century did science begin to catch up. The invention of the telescope made it possible for astronomers to study our nearest neighbors in space and it soon became clear that the widespread assumption that the sun and stars revolved around the earth was erroneous. Over the next hundred years the laws of physics, which govern the entire universe, were discovered, thanks in great measure to the work of Isaac Newton. By the nineteenth century insights into the mechanisms of genetics and the discovery that humans are descended from other animal species—a stupefying discovery in its time—began to take center stage in the scientific drama.

In the twentieth century Albert Einstein moved physics into a new phase, pointing out that our senses are unable to provide us with all knowledge and identifying a reality that can only be described in mathematical formulas. Since then we have learned more and more about what

93

took place when the universe was born, and what may happen in the future. Today we know quite well how long the universe has existed (some fifteen billion years), and we are beginning to sense the enormity of that universe, as it continues to expand. In recent decades we have come to understand the principles underpinning the structure of the cellular building blocks of life, and how our genetic matter is stored in the DNA molecule. We are also beginning to obtain deeper insights into how the smallest components of matter are constructed.

In some respects, these developments have moved the natural sciences closer to mysticism and Eastern religions. Phenomena are being studied today that cannot be directly experienced through our senses. These include:

+ The smallest particles of matter, so small that they will never be observable, even through the most sophisticated microscopes. At this size it is even difficult to determine what is matter and what is energy.
+ The size and expansion of the universe.
+ Events that occur at the speed of light.
+ The functions of the human brain.

These phenomena cannot be described so as to be comprehensible to our senses. For example, an electron that spins around the nucleus of an atom does not resemble a little ball revolving around a larger one, or a planet revolving around the burning sun. An electron is completely different. A whole new mode of abstract "thought" is required to be able even to approach these notions. Scientists, like mystics, have had to resort to symbols, imagery, and metaphors in their attempts to describe what cannot actually be experienced with our five senses.

If we examine the stories of the origins of all things through the prism of the knowledge we possess today, we will immediately realize that they cannot be literally accurate descriptions (although they may work very well as myths and symbols). Let us take a few examples from the Bible:

+ The earth is far older than the nearly six thousand years the Bible suggests.
+ The human species has evolved out of other animal species and so Adam must not have been made out of the dust of the ground or woman from his rib.

✦ The universe and everything in it was not created in six days.

✦ When Joshua wished to extend the length of the day in order to conquer the Amorites, he prayed to God to make the sun and moon stand still. In answer to his prayer "the sun stopped in midheaven, and did not hurry to set for about a whole day" (Joshua 10:13). Today we would write, "the earth stopped spinning for about a whole day."

The science of the human mind—modern psychology—has also developed over the course of the last hundred years. One of its main aims is to understand the aspects of the human psyche of which we are not directly aware. In this unconscious or subconscious part of our minds there are forgotten memories, the roots of needs that propel us in life, and instinctive thought patterns we have inherited. Some psychologists also claim that the need for meaning and security that gave rise to the notion of god(s) is to be found there as well. Others assert that knowledge of the human psyche may teach us more about the God who is hidden at the very center of our consciousness.

When science began to gain a foothold, the major religions felt their natural authority was being threatened and they reacted strongly. Christianity led the way, as it was the dominant religion in the countries where the great scientific discoveries were being made. If religious scriptures were found to contain errors, what would happen to the Christians' belief in an all-powerful God and in the Bible as divinely inspired or even "dictated" by God? Would the faithful lose their faith? Might religion simply collapse like a house of cards if the "inerrancy of scripture" card tottered?

The idea that some religious "facts" must be regarded as symbolic gradually came to be more accepted in most religions. God created the universe, but not in six days. God created humankind in God's image, but through evolution, thus allowing for the idea that human beings developed out of other animal species. In this way many people today have found a comfortable synthesis between religion and science, though religions have usually made the compromises in making room for scientific evidence within their theological beliefs. However, we must remain vigilantly aware that what we hold to be scientific "truths" today may have to be modified in the future.

For many religious people, the concern that religions might be rejected in light of increasing scientific knowledge seems, at least to some extent, justified. Just as some of the religious myths have had to make way for science, so God, too, may be superfluous in a world that is more and more readily explained on the basis of science. Widespread beliefs in the virtually complete ability of science to provide us with all the answers and in the only truth being knowledge that can be scientifically proven have developed a quasi-religious undertone.

Is God no longer necessary in a universe that may be explained through reason? Is it true that belief in the divine belongs to a more primitive stage of development we have now passed through? Or, on the contrary, will the instruments and methods of modern science enable us to obtain scientific proof of the existence of the divine? Or are none of these alternatives closest to the truth? Perhaps it is the case that scientifically provable facts can exist side by side with truths that are concealed and indescribable. I will elucidate these issues by discussing three modern sciences that have allowed us to approach the question of the existence and function of God in new ways: physics, biology, and psychology.

## ∽ 10

# The Encounter Between
# God and Contemporary Physics

THE IDEA that our universe came into being as a result of the Big Bang some fifteen billion years ago (at least ten and at most twenty, according to some sources) is generally accepted among scientists today, although there is still controversy about the details. At the initial moments of the Big Bang, the entire universe existed in a small area; in fact, it is now believed that this area was miniscule—much smaller than a pinhead. The universe then expanded rapidly, and after some time the stars and the planets came into being. Matter was created out of energy just as described in the formula developed by Einstein, $E = mc^2$, in which E stands for energy, m for mass and $c^2$ for the speed of light (300,000 kilometers per second) multiplied by itself. Enormous amounts of energy can thus be generated from very little matter, as we have seen in nuclear weapons. The expansion that began at the moment of the Big Bang has continued until the present and is ongoing still. The universe is in a state of continual enlargement.

A number of "laws" govern the universe. These for instance include:

*The law of gravity:* terrestrial bodies tend to fall toward the center of the earth.

*The laws that govern nuclear energy:* energy released by reactions within atomic nuclei, as in nuclear fission or fusion.

*The laws that govern electromagnetism:* the phenomena associated with electric and magnetic fields and their interactions with each other and with electric charges and currents.

*The laws of time and space:* the three spatial dimensions can be described as up/down, forward/backward, and sideways.

These laws arose out of the "conditions of origination," the special terms under which the universe was created at the first moments of the Big Bang. Had any of these original conditions or any of the laws of physics been even the slightest bit different, our universe would never have been able to come into being. They are perfectly suited to giving rise to the universe and life. Some of these prerequisites are described by the physicist Stephen Hawking:

+ Had the density of the developing universe been as little as one part in a thousand billion greater *or* less than it was, the universe would either have collapsed within ten years or been completely empty.
+ Had the universe, in the course of its development, expanded the least bit faster or more slowly, it would have collapsed. If the rate of expansion had been as little as 0.000000000000001 percent slower, the process would have failed and there would be no universe.
+ Had the mass of the particles of which atoms consist been only slightly different, the chemical elements that are the building blocks of nature would not have come into existence, so there would be neither nature nor human beings. Correspondingly, the life-giving sun and other stars would be unable to function if the charge of the electron had been only slightly different.[13]

It is astonishing that precisely these prerequisites were in place, thus permitting our universe to come into being, and that the laws of physics are so perfectly adapted to maintain it. Not disregarding the fact that if things had been otherwise we would not have been here to ask the questions, we must bear in mind that the probability of these extraordinarily optimum conditions arising by chance on the first try is virtually nonexistent. Michael Turner, another physicist, put it this way: "The precision is as if one could throw a dart across the entire universe and hit a bullseye one millimeter in diameter on the other side."

---

13. See for instance Stephen Hawking, *A Brief History of Time.*

## QUESTIONS ABOUT THE UNIVERSE

A number of questions may be posed in light of this understanding of the beginnings of the universe.

### What was there prior to the creation?

Our knowledge about the Big Bang is constantly increasing, and some scientists are of the opinion that the entire course of events has now been mapped out, down to the first fractions of a second. When the Big Bang took place, the universe probably "existed" in the form of an extremely small area, known as a "singularity." Interestingly, there is no time in a singularity. In light of this fact, we can conclude that the question asked above is probably formulated incorrectly. There was no "prior to the creation."

In earlier chapters we have mentioned the limitations of the human brain. We human beings are so accustomed to the concept of time that we cannot readily imagine that it has not always existed. Similarly, only a few hundred years ago it was difficult for people to conceive of the world as a round body revolving around the sun, because a very different impression was mediated to them by their senses.

It is of interest in this context that many religions, including Christianity, Islam, Judaism, Taoism, and Hinduism, have taken the stand that time only exists for the material reality of which human beings are a part, and that time came into being in conjunction with the creation. The divine, however, is "beyond time."

On the other hand, those of us who require a sense of order might counter that *something* must have existed before the creation of the universe with all its energy and matter. The answer is that the total amount of matter and energy in the universe is simply *nothing*. This is because there is exactly as much positive energy/matter as there is negative energy/matter in the universe. The sum total adds up to exactly 0. Thus we may establish that the religious thesis that the world was created out of nothing *(ex nihilo)* appears to be confirmed by science.

### How was it possible for a viable universe to be formed?

As described above, the prerequisite for the existence of the universe and the development of life is that the laws of physics are precisely regulated in accordance with certain principles. There are a couple of ways of explaining the apparently amazing coincidence that has allowed us to be where we are today. One is that our universe is not the only one that has existed. Many of these other universes may have been different with regard to the laws of nature, and thus were unable to go on existing or may not have the prerequisites to sustain life.

Where might these universes be? One possibility is that other universes have been formed and destroyed in the very spot where ours is now. Another is that a number of universes, with different laws, may exist beyond the bounds of the known universe, some ten billion light years away. A third is that there are other universes in existence in parallel with ours, but in different dimensions of space than the three known to us.

Thus it is possible that an infinite number of universes exist and have existed. Only in a few of them can intelligent life come into being, and we happen to be in one of those worlds, equipped with the capacity to pose questions regarding our own existence and God. In this way, the theory of many worlds is one possible explanation of the way in which exactly the "right" conditions for origination and laws of physics exist for our universe. This theory is in accord with the principle of natural selection that has led to the development of species, which means that the individuals with the best prerequisites are the ones who survived, while less well-adapted variants have become extinct.

We may regard the mystery of life on earth in accordance with the same principle. There are probably many millions of planets, among which there are occasional ones suitable for life. The problem arises when we attempt to apply this evolutionary principle to the universe, since we only know of one universe. Until we discover others, the theory of many universes remains no more than a hypothesis.

The other possible explanation is that there is only one universe, and it was created in precisely the right way so as to enable us to exist. This hypothesis is based on the understanding that there are laws and rules unknown to us that make it impossible for the universe to have any other form than the one it has and that this formulation of the universe coincides with the prerequisites for the development of intelligent life.

Obviously, we must then ask who or what decided that the universe was to have precisely the laws that enable us to exist. The most reasonable explanation is that an as-yet undefined principle provided these preconditions. Those who adhere to this hypothesis may call this principle "God."

*What is going to happen to the universe?*

Will the universe exist for all eternity? Maybe not. Some physicists believe that a number of billion of years from now the universe will cease to expand and begin to contract. This compression would conclude with another singularity (the Big Crunch). Subsequently, the cycle may be repeated, with a next Big Bang, an expanding universe, and so on. Other physicists disagree with this theory, and offer various hypotheses predicting different developments of the universe.

It was not science that introduced the idea that worlds are created and destroyed, created and destroyed, in an ever-repeating cycle. These ideas may be found in various ancient philosophical and religious systems. One is Hinduism, in which Brahma, the divine creator of the world, is considered to have a life cycle of some three hundred and eleven trillion years. Similar thoughts may be found in Buddhism. The first philosopher known to have put forward the idea of the existence of many different worlds was Anaximander, who lived in the sixth century BCE. Traditional forms of other religions, including Christianity, do not share this view. Rather, they consider the world to have been created once, in a unique event. Early Christian thought, however, like Jewish mysticism, reflects the view that our universe is only one of many created worlds.

## PHYSICS AND RELIGION

Clearly, many discoveries in physics and other sciences have contradicted the views of established religions. Thus it is not surprising that, according to recent studies, the number of scientists who believe in God is lower than the corresponding proportion of the general population. Increasing knowledge in the natural sciences seems to result in greater skepticism about the existence of a reality that can neither be experienced through our senses nor described in mathematical formulas.

Let us now examine the flip side of the coin and ask whether the sciences have come to conclusions that support some religious dogmas. Indeed there are ideas in religion that seem to be supported by the discoveries of scientists, such as the beliefs in a cyclic universe and in the existence of more than one universe, and the theories regarding the smallest components of matter. In his description of human development, Sufi poet Jalaluddin Rumi (1207–1273) comes close to contemporary knowledge of the process of evolution, which was not understood for another six hundred years: "Originally, you were clay. From being mineral, you became vegetable. From vegetable, you became animal, and from animal, man." It remains an open question whether these descriptions are to be regarded as true knowledge or simply as coincidences.

These points of contact do not touch directly on the core of religion, the divine. But in recent years, attempts have been made, for instance by physicists Frank Tipler and Paul Davies, to link discoveries in physics to the idea of a divine force, understood in terms of intelligence and consciousness. One such attempt is the Omega Point Theory, a term coined by theologian Pierre Teilhard de Chardin (1881–1955).

The Omega Point Theory is based on the idea that computers have become so sophisticated that in the near future there will be true artificial intelligence. Computers have also enabled us to create systems that can very closely imitate evolution and synthetic life. In the future, with more and more advanced data processing systems, we will probably be able to stimulate entire life systems. According to the Omega Point Theory, humanity will develop itself and artificially intelligent computers in such a way as to give rise to a kind of "superintellect" in the distant future many millions of years hence. If we see consciousness strictly scientifically, as a series of biochemical processes in the brain, there is no reason that advanced technology should not in the future enable us to simulate the mind of the individual human being. Then, in this distant future and using methods we cannot even so much as imagine today, we would be able to "resurrect" all human beings who have ever lived on earth. These risen individuals would then live eternal life in simulations that take place in computers with enormous capacities, in a kind of "virtual reality."

In the Omega Point Theory, the human community (or some eventual equivalent species) is the divine in the process of becoming.[14] God is what we, or rather our consciousnesses, will become one with in some distant future. Thus this theory coincides with the idea that all human beings bear the divine within themselves.

14. When Moses encountered God at the burning bush, he asked, "If I come to the Israelites and say to them, 'The God of your ancestors has sent me to you,' and they ask me, 'What is his name?' what shall I say to them?" God's reply to Moses was, "I am who I am" (Exodus 3:13–14). As the note in the NRSV indicates, an alternate interpretation is: "I will be what I will be."

Another hypothesis consistent with these theories that the world will be re-created in the form of a virtual reality in the unforeseeable future is the hypothesis of "the world as simulation." This idea is based on the thought that even now we may be part of some gigantic computer simulation. This theory holds that we came into being as the result of some advanced intelligence creating an artificial universe. The system is, then, so sophisticated that we experience ourselves as "real" in spite of the fact that we are just cogs in the wheels of some utterly ingenious piece of machinery.[15] Pursuant with this hypothesis, the divine might be the intelligence that built it—or, alternately, God too might be part of the created universe.

In this and similar ways, the natural sciences develop models and hypotheses that serve as potential explanations of what religions regard as concealed and indescribable. But hypotheses are the most physics can as yet produce.

---

15. Jewish mystics, too, have discussed the possibility that the world we believe we are living in is not the real world. The Torah, the five books of Moses, is then presented as proof that we are actually living in the real world.

# ⌁ 11

## *God and Biology*

ACCORDING TO CURRENT scientific thought, the sun and the planets were created approximately five billion years ago, and the very first forms of life appeared three to four billion years ago. These were relatively simple life forms, out of which the first cells developed and went on to join, multiply, and give rise to the first simple multicellular organisms. Thus the first plants that used photosynthesis to obtain energy came into being. These forms of life gave rise in turn to cells that were able to acquire solar energy indirectly, by consuming plant cells. Animals arose out of these simple beings. The first were very primitive, and then became increasingly complex. *Homo sapiens* is the most complex species to have come into being, as far as we know. This complexity is mainly due to the development of well-functioning brains, enabling the unique capacities of analysis, memory, and communication.

A cell consists of an outer membrane, under which the cytoplasm is located. Inside the cytoplasm is the core, or nucleus of the cell, which is surrounded by an inner membrane. The nucleus contains genetic matter, DNA, which is made up of relatively uncomplicated units but is able to house all our genes. This is a daunting task, as we have some thirty thousand of them. These genes provide the patterns for the development of proteins that enable the cell to function.

A cell may be compared to an extraordinarily complex machine, containing millions of small structures that have to be functional if the cell is to work optimally. One astonishing fact is that every human being is made up of some fifty trillion cells. If the cells from one single adult human being were laid out in a long chain, it would encircle the earth no less than twelve times. All these trillions of cells, each of which in its turn contains millions of components, work in highly sophisticated collaboration. Furthermore, our planet is home to several billion people who interact with one another, with other animal species, and with the natural surroundings. At the same time, all the components in nature interact in a web so complex it boggles the human mind.

And yet, although we cannot really conceive of it, this elaborate system that is our earth is one huge interacting unit, every aspect of which is interdependent. In science, these connections are referred to as "chaos phenomena." Briefly, this idea holds that one original event, which may appear insignificant in its context, ultimately comes to have enormous consequences because it gives rise to an unending chain reaction. One metaphor for this is the picture of a butterfly fluttering its wings in New York and thereby initiating a chain of events that eventually results in a hurricane in Beijing. Interestingly, this idea applies not to certain selected events, but to *everything* that happens.

One illustration of this concept is the question of what would have happened if Adolf Hitler had been accepted to the Vienna Art Academy in his youth. In all likelihood world history would have taken a different course. The Second World War would not have happened, or at least not in the way it did. Millions of people would not have died in the war and would have given rise to progeny, whereas others would not have had children with the partners they now did. Furthermore, for a particular individual to be born into our world one particular sperm out of many million has to be the first to reach one particular egg cell. If the instant of conception is shifted by as little as a few minutes, the individual created will be a different one. One of the consequences would thus be that the vast majority of people born in the last fifty years would never have come into being, although there would have been other individuals instead of them.

Another example is a person who does not answer the phone when it starts to ring as she is leaving home. Because she does not answer, she bumps into a friend on the street and thus the friend happens not to be killed by an automobile a few minutes later. This friend thus does not die, and so has the opportunity to affect the lives of thousands of other people who, in turn, have an impact on the lives of millions of others. Furthermore, the children she lives to have will directly and indirectly come to influence an infinite number of other people in a never-ending chain.

It may seem that certain specific powerful individuals are those who determine the course of history, but this is not the case. Every human being has an impact, directly and indirectly, on what the future will be. We all influence the development of our world: we just do not know what the waves of events triggered by our actions *look like* as they spread slowly across the earth. It is not a matter of *us and them,* of *this and that.* Everything is one vast unit, just as religions have always taught.

## LIFE ON EARTH

In the previous chapter the physical preconditions required for the creation of the universe were discussed. Science has also shown that an amazing number of biological preconditions were necessary to make life on earth possible. Had they only been a tiny bit different, there would have been no life. Naturally, we ask how such astonishing precision managed to happen. If we disregard the option of random chance (which has been calculated as negligible), there are a few conceivable explanations, two of which are the most probable and are not mutually exclusive:

+ We are a consequence of the fact that our planet, of many millions of conceivable planets, happened to have the appropriate conditions for life.
+ We have come into being as a result of biological principles that strive inexorably in the direction of the creation of life.

Let us examine these two explanations in somewhat greater detail.

### Our planet happened to have the preconditions for life

The universe consists of some one hundred billion galaxies, or collections of stars, each of which contains some two hundred billion solar systems. Some of these solar systems have planets that could, theoretically, maintain life. In order for life to arise, there are a number of factors that have to be perfectly adjusted, so perfectly that most planets remain uninhabitable and void of life.

Some of the preconditions that have to be fulfilled in order for life (in the sense we normally give to the word) to come into being on a planet include:

+ *Temperature.* For life to exist, there must be water in solid, liquid, and gaseous forms, which requires exact temperatures. The distance from the sun to the perimeter of the solar system is some six thousand million kilometers and life can only arise inside an area some ten million kilometers wide, precisely where the earth is located in our solar system.
+ *Size.* If a planet is to be able to utilize gravity to retain its water, it must be a certain size. The earth fulfills this condition.
+ *The content of the atmosphere.* The atmosphere extends some three to ten thousand kilometers above the surface of the earth. If there is no atmosphere, or if the atmosphere has the wrong proportions of oxygen, carbon dioxide, and nitrogen there can be no life. For example, all the vegetation on a planet would be annihilated if the concentration of oxygen were higher than the 21 percent we have on our earth, because fires would be unable to self-extinguish. In its turn, the composition of the atmosphere of the earth is a result of an intricate interplay among plants, animals, and microorganisms (such as bacteria). We exhale the carbon dioxide needed by plants and plants produce the oxygen our metabolism requires.

Because there is probably an enormous number of planets in the universe, it is reasonable to imagine that some of them satisfy these prerequisites, though we do not yet know whether other planets that do fulfill the conditions have given rise to life.

### Biological principles give rise to the conditions for life

Just as there are physical principles that are conditions for life, there are also biological principles that regulate all living organisms. The principles of procreation, which include the laws of genetics and natural selection constitute one such example. These biological laws made it possible for all the animal species, including *Homo sapiens,* to come into being. There are also principles governing specific bodily functions, such as the immune system, the formation and growth of embryos, and the brain. Principles of biology also prevail at the cellular level, governing phenomena such as the production of proteins, cell multiplication, and cell death.

The principles of reproduction, like all biological principles, are ingenious. Over millions of years, the species have undergone mutation through tiny changes in the genetic matter to produce new types of plants and animals. Only the species with the best qualifications for survival or with the capacity to populate a niche in nature have endured in the long term. Thus development has moved in the direction of increasingly complex, sustainable species. The development of the sexes was a major break-through, since mixing the genes from two individuals for the formation of offspring brought a vastly increased potential for diversity.

Evidently these changes have not taken place in a steady stream, but through a series of steps. Over the course of millions of years, the earth would be dominated by certain species of flora and fauna until evolutionary developments suddenly took a leap, with new species appearing and some old ones dying out. Although there are many hypotheses for these leaps in development, the real causes have not yet been explained.

Through this process, nature has created humankind, the species with the greatest intelligence, and probably the only one able to ask questions about the reasons for our own existence. This does not mean that we are the species that will, in the long term, be the one to survive. *Homo sapiens* has now existed for some two hundred thousand years, while certain types of insects have been around two hundred times longer. Some simple plant forms, such as grass, have been on earth much longer.

Today we take biological principles more or less for granted. This makes it all the more important to remind ourselves occasionally of the tremendously intricate development process that produced *Homo sapiens* and of all the things that could have gone haywire along the way. For example, for life to be able to continue, the very first life forms on earth had to be self-generating. This in itself requires elaborate machinery. Somehow the transfer of complex information from generation to generation had to be in place from the very outset. In other words, there was a threshold life had to cross in order to be able to reproduce. Although scientists have been able to prove that simple organic compounds, such as those out of which proteins and DNA are built, could be created under conditions that prevailed on earth three to four billion years ago, it is an enormous step from there to self-generating cell-like forms of life and it is clear from calculations that the probability of this threshold being crossed is small indeed. Furthermore, if DNA had been slightly more or less predisposed to mutate, life as we know it would not have been developed.

Equally astonishing is the extraordinarily complex structure of the cell, the human body, and the nature we interact with. Some scientists assert that the principles of evolution, as we understand them today, can explain the fact that three to four billion years sufficed to give rise to these biological structures, while others claim that the rapid development cannot be explained by these principles alone.

Likewise, it has been shown that all of humanity originated from a small number of individuals. If this little group of human beings who populated our earth some two hundred thousand years ago had, for some reason, died out, it is probable that the most intelligent animal species today would be the apes.

Another facet of the marvelous and perilous development of *Homo sapiens* to keep in mind is that single cell microorganisms are highly successful at reproduction. For instance, there are many million more of this form of life than of insects and many billion more single cell organisms than mammals. Why, then, is nature so structured as to promote the development of increasingly complex life forms, including plants, animals, and human beings?

In spite of their enormous complexity, biological organisms may have developed out of a small number of laws and principles that are functional in the sense that they are the source for the creation of increasingly capable and complex organisms. It is not certain that the principles of evolution put forward by Darwin and Wallace suffice to explain this entire, fantastic development. There may, for instance, be as yet undiscovered principles that contribute to the increasing intricacy of nature. It may not be necessary to use the divine as the explanation for all that science has been unable to explain to date. The conviction that there remain unknown principles of biology can also be used to explain other riddles such as:

+ How can the fertilized egg cell contain all the information that governs the development of the embryo toward the birth of a new individual?
+ How can a mere ten thousand genes contain all the innate information for instinctive behavior that enables, for example, migratory birds to fly thousands of miles with incredible precision and exactitude?
+ How can we explain the development of human consciousness by the existence of as small a number as some thirty thousand genes? The human brain has been estimated to contain approximately one

hundred billion cells, each of which, in turn, is in contact with some ten thousand other nerve cells. The potential variation for how a thought may be formulated is thus indescribably large.

In the future, science will be able to answer these questions and some of the answers are sure to be astonishing indeed. There are principles and laws of nature still waiting to be discovered, but that does not mean they are supernatural. We must not forget that the universe has existed for billions of years, but modern science only for a few hundred. If beings capable of thinking analytically remain on our earth, the future will see tremendous progress toward understanding the phenomena we still consider inexplicable today.

A century ago, the very idea that medicines could cure infectious diseases and cancer was inconceivable. Twenty-five years ago we could not imagine what the computers we use today would be capable of achieving. A mere fifteen years ago the ongoing information dissemination revolution was beyond most of our wildest dreams. There is no way we can know today what developments will take place within the coming century, not to mention the coming thousand, ten thousand, one hundred thousand, or million years—and the universe may well exist for billions of years into the future. We must rein in our hubris and recognize that the individuals of the future will regard us as having been virtually illiterate in terms of knowledge. If we can acknowledge that most questions will be answered in the future, perhaps we will also see that we do not need to fill in every single blank in our knowledge repertoire with God and mysticism.

It does appear clear, however, that the principles regulating nature are watertight. They do not need to be governed, monitored, or maintained by any external force. Still, the question remains of where these extraordinarily functional biological principles came from to begin with. Was it mere coincidence or was there "something" that initially established the rules and initiated the process?

## ৴ 12

# A God in the Depths
# of Our Consciousness?

RELIGIONS TELL US that we may find God through an
inner search in our own minds. Over the past century, we have come to know more and more about how the human mind
works. Can this knowledge lead us to insights as to whether or not the
divine exists at the core of each individual's mental and emotional world?
What can the science of psychology teach us regarding the question of
whether or not there may be a God?

## THE HUMAN PSYCHE

To make a very simple analogy, the human psyche is like a multistory
house. The aspect of our psyche of which we are conscious is the top floor,
and contains many of our memories and thoughts. When we speak, we
normally do so with the conscious part of our personality. We also experience our feelings and fantasies in this part of our psyche. Our logical
thought processes and our direct decision-making procedures likewise
take place at the conscious levels of our psyche. It is in this area that we
become aware that we have a personality, an ego.

The other stories of the house are ones of which we are unaware, the
subconscious floors. One of them houses our personal subconscious. This
aspect of the psyche contains personal memories, feelings, and experiences to which our memories do not have immediate access, but which
may still radically affect the way in which we live our lives. When we react
in affect—when we fall in love, are angry, unhappy, or provoked—unconscious or forgotten aspects of our psyche are often activated. Even our

rational thought processes may be affected by the subconscious aspects of our psyche.

On the next flight down, we find structures of the psyche shared by all human beings, including our instincts and our drives, as well as universal patterns of imagination and primordial images or symbols.

The house itself was designed by two primary architects. One is the heredity inherent in our genes, the characteristics we inherit from our parents. The other main architect is our previous experience. Everything we have experienced has an impact on and colors our reactions and attitudes throughout our lives. There is general consensus that early childhood experiences mark our personalities. The question as to the extent to which nature and nurture, respectively, play into the creation of our personalities is still an open one.

## SIGMUND FREUD

Sigmund Freud is regarded as the physician responsible for the major breakthrough in our understanding of the importance of the subconscious to personality, although it should be recalled that some philosophers, religious leaders, and scientists prior to Freud also took an interest in trying to understand how the mind works.

What was the position of this founding father of modern psychology with regard to God? Freud referred to himself as an atheist. He was of the opinion that God is, above all, a projection of the father figure human beings need in order to maintain a sense of being protected, the kind of protection a small child seeks from parents. Freud pointed out that the characteristics of the personal God described in the Bible and elsewhere are congruent with the characteristics children attribute to a father, not least in their contradictory respects. The God of the Hebrew scriptures is at once strict, just, judgmental, loving, biased, demanding, and generous. Freud thus rejected the idea of a personal God with human attributes, which he viewed as the attempts of individuals to create security for themselves through a father figure who governs an otherwise incomprehensible and fearsome world. According to Freud, identifying the frightening forces of nature with human traits is our way of attempting to bring the uncontrollable under control. When misfortune strikes, we try to find meaning in existence and an explanation for suffering. Freud went on to reject the idea of a life after death as the inability of the individual to accept the implacable nature of death.

Freud also explained away the feelings of the mystics of being at one with the universe as a regression to the period in infancy when the human individual has not yet learned to distinguish between the self and the rest of the world. He described newborns as not knowing where they themselves end and the surrounding world begins and experiencing everything, including the mother, as part of one and the same reality.

Freud described religion as one gigantic illusion, a global neurosis. Although in his last book Freud did allow that he had not necessarily discovered the entire truth regarding the inherent force that gave rise to religions, he never explicitly stated any belief in the divine. This standpoint on religious experience was Freud's way of shutting the door to the house of the psyche, thus turning it into a personal refuge for our thoughts, instincts, and emotions, for which each individual bears full personal responsibility.

## CARL GUSTAV JUNG

Another figure in the foreground of the development of psychology and a contemporary of Freud, Carl Gustav Jung, also rejected the personal God of Christianity. From that stance, however, he went on to analyze religion, stressing the gnostic mystical traditions. Freud and Jung were initially colleagues and close friends, but eventually broke with each other.

One of several reasons for his separation from Freud's work was that Jung was firmly convinced that the house of the psyche contained a skylight to eternity. In his view, one inherent aspect of humanity is divine (the Self) and stands in direct contact with the universe and thus with the hidden, indescribable God. At the very depths of every human being lies the possibility of encountering the great mystery designated by religions with names such as the inner treasury, Atman, and God. This aspect of the psyche cannot be described in words, since words simply do not suffice. The only way to become aware of its existence is through personal experience. The mystical experience takes place when these aspects of the human unconscious force their way up to the level of consciousness.

According to Jung, every individual is unique and has a particular inherent potential. The main life task of each of us is to develop this potential to the full by attaining insights into our inner world and striving to integrate the various aspects of our personality into a whole. This makes it possible also to acknowledge our evil sides and thus to better control them. Like the mystical forms of monotheistic religions and like Eastern religions, Jung held the view that we have to be released from the restrictions of the ego in order to accomplish fully the ultimate aim, contact with the Self. This view coincides with, for instance, the Sufi thought that "I looked into my own heart. In that place, I saw him. He was in no other place."

A human being who makes contact with the Self within becomes both wiser and more ethical. Freud and Jung agreed that a human being who develops and matures leaves behind the symbolic, personal notion of God, but one of the important points on which they differed was that Freud asserted that this enabled the individual to become liberated from the need to believe in God, while Jung regarded inner maturity as an opening to the insight that we all bear the divine within us.

Jung also elucidated ways in which it is possible to reach these deep levels of the human psyche. Like religious traditions, these methods require the assistance of a mentor, in this case a specially trained psychotherapist. Jung was also of the view that although the existence of the Self cannot be scientifically proven, it does exist. Critics of Jung take this claim as a point of departure for asserting that he thus abandoned science for religion.

## PSYCHOLOGY AND GOD

Recent scientific research on religions has proffered psychological and physiological explanations of nearly all the phenomena of religion and religious experiences, thus expounding on almost every aspect of religion without having to refer to either alternative realities or divine forces. According to these findings, everything, including the experience of the divine, may be attributed to biochemical processes in the brain. For example:

✦ The personal God who provides our security in an unruly world may be rooted in the experience of parents or of other caretakers who, when we were children, gave us warmth, love, and nurturing, and instilled in us a belief that, in the great scheme of things, all will be well.

✦ Meditative experiences of the divine may be explained as images and symbols from the unconscious breaking through to consciousness in states of meditation when we close off our thought processes and sensory impressions and place ourselves in a passive state of receptivity. In doing so, we abolish the barriers that normally distinguish the unconscious from our conscious thoughts. In a crisis situation, when external reality and our inner experiences are in conflict, the brain may choose to trust in subjective inner impressions. Similarly, a brain subjected to hallucinogenic drugs or psychiatric illness may be a helpless hostage to powerful experiences that penetrate the conscious mind.

✦ The human need to understand the world we live in may result in "supernatural" interpretations. In a pre-scientific age, the only way people could explain some of the phenomena of nature was to believe there were gods. Although we have learned more and more about the natural sciences, human beings today still have this need. It is as essential today as it was in the past to be able to explain the dark sides of life, including suffering, pain, grief, and death.

✦ Religion may offer us means of controlling a life situation in which we otherwise feel helpless. Just as people in the past turned to God in the hope of influencing the forces of nature, we may pray to God today to help us in times of need. Religion may also offer compensation for suffering in this life in terms of the hope of a better situation in the life to come.

✦ All human beings need goals and meaning in life for their mental health. If the "ordinary" world cannot satisfy these needs, we may seek other ways of finding a path for our journey through life. Religious experiences are known to coincide frequently with life crises. A religious world view offers explanations for why we exist, where we are headed, and how we should live to achieve the ultimate goal.

In this way every description of subjective religious experience may be said to show that religion satisfies basic human needs. Just as we require nourishment, love, and security to develop as individuals, we also need spirituality. In this view, God is nothing more than a biochemical signal in the brain. This way of reasoning can either provide a point of departure for a rejection of the idea of God or a belief that spiritual needs fill an invaluable function for humankind. According to the latter view a person who has neither religion nor spirituality is an incomplete individual. Jung saw the basic problem of an individual in a psychological crisis as being the absence of a religious/spiritual view of the world. Without spirituality the human being deteriorates. Without belief in a superior meaning in life, the human community may dissolve.

Those who claim to be atheists may, in line with this view, be forced to replace traditional religion and notions of god(s) with a more scientific or material religion. Those who put forward this view claim, for instance, that Freud personally replaced the need for spirituality with a more or less "religious" belief in the subconscious, and repressed sex drives as the cause of psychiatric disorders.

There are endless examples of how religion has been abused: crusades, religious oppression, sectarian suicide, and terrorist attacks are merely a few. On countless occasions, faith has shown itself capable of developing into obsession and fanaticism, resulting for many in the rejection of religion and everything having to do with belief in God. However, the human need for spirituality is a highly complex phenomenon, as we have seen, and not all aspects of this need can be explained by a single cause. We must go on to ask ourselves whether some aspects of religious faith may only originate in the human psyche, while others relate to "objective" truths.

How can we know whether a religious experience is real? How, for instance, can we distinguish between a mentally ill person's experience of reality and the visions of a prophet or the founder of a religion? In many respects they may be similar. Would the prophets of the Hebrew scriptures or the historical saints be considered mentally deviant if they preached their truths today? How can we know that the hallucinations resulting from the use of certain drugs are not just as true as the inner visions of the mystics? The answer is that we cannot be certain.

Such experiences may result in misery and destruction or, alternatively, in inner maturity, wisdom, and a solid ethical foundation. One possible explanatory model is thus that inner visions and experiences that result in injury to the individual and the surrounding world are not based on the innermost truths of religion. Another is that all spiritual experience is true, but only individuals who are able to put such experiences into a constructive context can use them as part of a process of inner maturation, while experiences that cannot be integrated into a constructive model have negative consequences. Representatives of the mystical traditions of various religions have always been aware of this and have concurred that it is dangerous to undertake the inward search without guidance. The path from faith to knowledge is paved with risks.

Many psychologists of religion stress that descriptions of the psychological and physiological explanations of religious phenomena are not judgments of whether or not these phenomena are real. Psychology, like physics and biology, may provide scientific explanations of many of the great puzzles of existence, but it cannot provide us with answers to the questions about the actual organization of reality or the existence of God. The observation that the idea of God satisfies many human needs is no proof either of the existence of God or the opposite. Every feeling our brain experiences corresponds to a biological event. This fact, however, makes those feelings neither more nor less true. Just as physics and biology are governed by material laws that do not require the intervention of a God, there will always be psychological and physiological explanations for a mental experience of the divine. Perhaps the system is perfect, in which case science will not require the existence of a God in order to explain our internal and external worlds. This does not contradict the idea that God exists and is the cause and basis of all things.

It has been shown that a subjective sense of the existence of God results, for many people, in a greater state of psychological well-being, and that experiencing this sensation can result in inner development. This positive development will depend both on the human being in question and on the religious culture within which the search arises. Thus positive consequences of human experiences of God are not contingent upon providing an objective answer to the question of whether or not the divine exists.

Experiences resulting from meditation may be regarded in a corresponding way, and may either be described negatively, in terms of regression (a return to the way the infant experienced the world), or positively, in terms of recovery and reuse of early brain functions. In conjunction with the ability of the adult brain to structure information, this may pave the way for expanding our experience of reality.

It has been a problem for some experts in the psychology of religion to distinguish between their own religious values (often deeply rooted in the personality) and scientific facts relating to a sphere that is supposed, by definition, to be "beyond reality." Apparently scientific theories may be based on a solidly cemented foundation of personal opinion and experience. Jung was obviously correct in perceiving that the experience of God can neither be confirmed nor denied using scientific methods. When push comes to shove it is all about subjective experience, which we may choose either to reject or accept.

The subjective existence of an image of God in the human consciousness is a fact, and psychologists are unanimous in stating that in psychological respects God is a reality and may even be a necessity. However, the question still remains as to whether God exists outside the human psyche, in objective reality.

## ∽ 13

## *God and Science: A Few Conclusions*

SCIENCE STRIVES to split reality into tiny pieces in order to analyze and describe it. This analysis translates reality into a language that enables us to communicate about it. This language is based, in its turn, on our senses, the links between human consciousness and the world around us, and enables us to describe reality objectively. Still, we must always bear in mind that the five senses are the entire toolbox through which we can perceive external reality, and scientific methods only allow us to describe it in fragmented form.

According to religion, if we are to comprehend divine reality, we must do precisely the opposite. We must disregard our senses and refrain from analysis. We are not to examine the parts but experience the whole. Religion and science thus attempt to describe the world from diametrically opposed points of view.

Can science aid us in our religious search by clarifying the questions that are to be asked and liberating them from superstition and overly literal faith? Could science even be a path to insight into the divine, or is it a *cul-de-sac* in the search for God?

In my personal view, the strongest scientific argument for the functioning of an unexplained force in the universe is the fact that the world we live in satisfies all the requirements that enable life to exist in it. The laws of the universe are consistent throughout the universe. Every law that holds true in our galaxy will hold true in galaxies light years distant. The laws of physics have been unchanged since creation and will remain immutable in the future as well. Similarly, the principles of biology are consistent, at least in the part of the universe with which we are familiar.

The structure of the cell, the production of proteins, and the function of DNA are, in principle, identical for a germ and a human being.

A person who does not believe in God will claim that we would not be here to discuss the matter without precisely the right conditions for the existence of the universe and the origin of life. Two of the reasonable explanatory models are that the conditions were "tailor made" for this particular universe and, alternately, that our universe is merely one of an infinite number of universes. If the latter is correct, our current knowledge regarding what reality actually "looks like" is apparently so limited as to prevent us from drawing any safe conclusions as to the non-existence of God.

We do not know where the laws of nature come from or whether they had a creator. What we do know is that no eventual God violates these laws (or at least not very often). Those who do not believe in God may claim that the "laws of nature" are sufficient to explain how everything came into being. A few principles of physics and biology are able to explain the entire process of development, from the creation of the universe down to the amazing single cell, and from there to plants and to the extraordinarily complex species of animals on earth today. According to this view, nature and the laws of nature provide a satisfactory explanation of all life.

This is a circular argument, since no eventual God is required to be visible in any other way than precisely through these laws. Although the theory of evolution is a likely explanatory model for the origin of all life, there is no proof that it provides the full answer. For example, the laws of evolution do not explain their own existence. If a person chooses not to believe in stories about miracles, God has never once been revealed other than in that which every human being can experience all around and inside him- or herself. The system is perfect and everything runs like one gigantic piece of "machinery." The question remains whether God created it, "exists in" it, or "is" it. We might also ask: can we agree with the *Tao Te Ching* that "Man takes his law from the Earth; the Earth takes its law from Heaven; Heaven takes its law from the Tao"?

One forceful scientific argument against the existence of a concealed God, in my view, is the hypothesis that mystical divine insights are a return to experiences of infancy, when the boundary lines with the surrounding world are effaced. The next question is then whether the experiences of the little child represent real contact with the divine, a contact we lose as we grow older, or whether they are merely the self-absorbed misconceptions about reality of an as yet not fully developed brain.

Science has provided an interesting piece of evidence with the discovery that the brain of an infant is more developed than that of the adult in one respect, which is that the child has twice as many of the links between brain cells that enable "thought" as the adult, and that many disappear around the same time we acquire language. Perhaps it is the case that at the time we give names to the things around us, we lose a different, inborn ability—in which case the interesting question is what that ability might be.

Let us speculate that the answer is that our capacity to perceive the whole, an ability we carry with us from birth, is lost to us as children when we strive to structure sensory experience into thoughts and express them as words. If so, after we lose our inherent ability to experience reality we must then spend the rest of our lives painfully attempting to regain it. Perhaps it is no coincidence, then, that in our efforts to restore our relationship to this reality we become like infants again, turning inward, toward ourselves, effacing our adult egos and liberating ourselves from the language we normally use to explain reality. Perhaps the words of Jesus, "Truly I tell you, unless you change and become like children, you will never enter the kingdom of heaven" (Matthew 18:3), and the words of the *Tao Te Ching*, "He who has in himself abundantly the attributes (of the Tao) is like an infant," confirm Freud's assertion, but in a different way than he perceived. Perhaps, perhaps not. The answer to this question is somewhere deep inside the consciousness of the little child. In spite of all the progress of science, we are unable to reveal the answer to this mystery.

Psychology and religion share a belief in the idea that there are depths of consciousness within each of us to which we do not have instant access. Everything is there, but we must learn to penetrate the bastions of defense preventing our conscious selves from achieving contact with the levels of insight, knowledge, and wisdom that are alive within us.

## GOD AND RATIONAL THINKING

Will some of the unsolved riddles of science remain unsolved forever? Will God eventually be the answer of last resort with regard to the creation of the universe and of human life? Personally, I do not believe that science will have to use God as the explanation of most of the as yet unsolved riddles of life and the universe. We are going to find many answers in the future. Einstein also indicated this belief when he said, "The most unintelligible thing about the universe is that it is intelligible."

However, science will not be able to provide all the answers. As early as the 1930s, mathematician Kurt Gödel proved that certain questions will never be able to be answered in scientific formulas or experiments. And Werner Karl Heisenberg, a physicist experimenting with the smaller components of matter, proved that we will never attain full knowledge of every phenomenon in the universe. It is not possible to distinguish completely the observer from the observed (that is, the world around us), which means that our interpretation of the reality all around us will always be subjective and colored.

Some events will thus *always* elude full scientific scrutiny and proof. It is simply not true that the only thing that exists is that which can be scientifically proven. Science must question and reject anything that can be refuted, but science does not have the right to reject what cannot be proven.[16] While it is the mission of every scientist to seek the answers to the mysteries of the universe, each of us must also accept, with humility, our own limits—and so must religion. As C. J. Jung put it: "The ethics of a scientist command him to admit where his knowledge ends. This end is the beginning of wisdom."

Is, then, the divine an area that will never be open to scientific analysis or proof? Will there or will there not be some sudden scientific discovery through which God is revealed? Turning the question around, will the science of the future succeed in refuting the existence of God?

If humankind survives, there is a great deal that speaks in favor of the idea that development and collection of knowledge will proceed to levels we cannot imagine even in our wildest dreams today. Therefore it is impossible to predict what discoveries and surprises scientists will come up with in the future. We cannot say, with any certainty whatsoever, that

---

16. It can be asserted, as an extension of this argument, that anything whose existence cannot be refuted could exist—for instance, elves, dragons, and trolls. It does appear reasonable that if these creatures that mythology describes as having regularly been observed by human beings do exist, then modern scientific methods would have verified their existence. However, in the name of consistency, perhaps we must be open-minded and not reject the hypothesis that they do exist (although personally I must admit that I find it improbable).

in the future the divine will fall within the realm of what human beings are able to understand. However, we must not disregard the possibility that future science will enable us to understand more and more about God.

There is one other matter that should be brought up in this context, and that relates back to the thesis purported by some mystics that God becomes self-aware through humankind. In the immenseness of the universe, so enormous we cannot possibly embrace its scope with our minds, intelligent life has arisen on (at least) one little planet. The organic forms of life we refer to as human are endowed with the fantastic ability to use their senses and their consciousness to study the universe of which they are one small part. In this way, through the little creatures on the tiny planet we call earth in the galaxy we denote as the Milky Way, one of a hundred billion galaxies, the universe is becoming aware of itself. If there is no life on any other planets, then nature has, in this one single place and during this relatively short epoch, become aware of itself through human beings. This may be what the mystics mean when they assert that the divine, which permeates the entire universe, has attained self-awareness through humankind.

Before we leave the sciences, let us end with a narrative from the Talmud, the collection of Jewish law and traditions, that alludes to the high value God places on human rational thinking.

In a legal disputation with his colleagues, Rabbi Eliezer found himself unable to persuade his fellow scholars that his view was correct. In his frustration, he asserted that the carob tree outside would prove that he was right. The tree uprooted itself and moved a hundred cubits but his colleagues said, "Proof cannot be brought from a tree." Then Rabbi Eliezer went on to claim that the water in the stream would prove he was right, and the waters began to flow backward, but his colleagues responded that water was not proof. After trying once more with the walls of the house, which, quite rightly, began to bulge, but still failing to persuade his colleagues, Rabbi Eliezer cried out that God should decide. A voice was heard from heaven saying: "Why do you not listen to Rabbi Eliezer? Can you not see that the law supports his view?" Whereupon Rabbi Joshua arose and proclaimed, "The Torah is no longer in heaven! The Law was given to us by God, and the Law says that decisions should be made in accordance with the majority. So we need no longer pay attention to voices from heaven." According to the Talmud, God was perfectly satisfied with this position in favor of reason.

*~ Part V*

A Concealed God?

## ᴄ 14

# *Is There a God?*
# *Arguments and Counterarguments*

UNTIL ABOUT A CENTURY AGO, very few people would state openly that they did not believe there was a God. Although one of the explanations for this reticence probably lay in a fear of offending established institutions, the vast majority of people basically regarded the existence of a deity as a fact—a given, an unquestioned truth. Most people took the existence of God for granted in the same way they accepted that the sun shone in the sky. Similarly, we know of hardly any societies or cultures since the beginning of time that did not believe in some metaphysical power.

Today, although there are still many people who are religious and who believe in God, more and more individuals, particularly in Western societies, have become skeptical about the existence of a deity. Many in the Western world refer to themselves as atheists and others as agnostics who are unable or unwilling to take a definite position on whether or not there is a God.

Is it possible to *argue* the existence or non-existence of God, to take a stand on something so completely intangible? Some representatives of religion have attempted to "prove" the existence of God, but scrutiny of such proof has consistently been its downfall. The conclusions drawn by atheists regarding the absence of a God also have their shortcomings. Let us nevertheless examine some of the arguments put forward both for and against.

## SOME ARGUMENTS
## AGAINST THE EXISTENCE OF GOD

### *If there is a God, why is there evil and suffering?*

In our world we see much to rejoice in, but we also see a great deal of suffering. People fall ill or are injured or killed in accidents; many others suffer starvation or violence. Our nearest and dearest may abandon or betray us. At times our life can feel meaningless. We may also grieve, or feel dispirited, for no apparent reason.

Humans are complex beings. We do good deeds, we help others, and we can show respect. However, we also do evil: we betray others, we injure or hurt even those we love, we cause great suffering through our neglect and lack of care. Some deeds that do harm to others are not driven by ill-intent, but are lacking in consideration. In committing evil deeds we injure other human beings, animals, or nature, the very prerequisite for all life. Clearly, humankind is both good and evil, leading us to ask: If there is a God, how can this God accept all the suffering and evil in the world? Is such a God worthy of the name?

One of the instruments used in Christianity to counteract this argument is the concept of "the devil," a being who is powerful but subordinate to God. Thus evil is situated outside God, and God can remain purely good. Every human being possesses free will, the ability to choose his or her deeds. This is each person's inner struggle; the choice between doing good and bad. The idea of evil and good as two independent forces was taken to its extreme in Zoroastrianism, founded nearly three thousand years ago, but with relatively few practitioners today.

Similar ideas are expressed in Hindu mythology, where gods represent good and demons evil. These forces are in combat, both against one another and, sometimes, on the side of or against humankind. It is the task of the individual to choose between good and evil, and that choice generates positive or negative karma.

Traditional Judaism has a complex picture of God. God is just, but a harsh judge. People, in their turn, have to make choices, such as the one between good and evil, that allow them to grow and develop. God's words to Cain provide a pertinent example: "If thou doest not well, sin coucheth at the door; and unto thee is its desire, but thou mayest rule over it" (Genesis 4:7).

Not everyone, however, is prepared to accept these explanations of why there is evil. Those who regard God as representing the highest ideal also ask how such a model can condone the suffering of human beings. Those who conceive of God as being personal, omnipotent, omniscient, loving, and good may find it particularly difficult to solve the problem of the existence of evil.

Both monotheistic mysticism and Eastern religions put forward the idea that if there were no evil, we would not have to choose—but this would also prevent us from choosing good. They also suggest that good can emerge from evil, since suffering is often the impetus for insight and growth. The view that crises help us to gain insight into the great scheme of things is held not only by some schools of religious thought, but also by schools of philosophy and psychology. Viktor Frankl (1905–1997), a psychiatrist who studied with Freud and who was incarcerated in concentration camps for three years during World War II, wrote: "When a man finds that it is his destiny to suffer, he will have to accept his suffering as his task; his single and unique task. . . . His unique opportunity lies in the way in which he bears his burden."

In one of the Buddhist worlds there are demigods who live in harmony and without evil. This world, however, contains none of the challenges and growth opportunities of human life, no crises. As opposed to human beings, demigods are unable to achieve insight or enlightenment. All they can do is exist, and they are said to envy human beings, who are able to accumulate wisdom and positive karma by living good lives. The relationship between angels and human beings is similarly described in Judaism. As opposed to angels, human beings may sanctify the divine. And in Hinduism, the lower deities are said to desire to be reborn as human beings so as to be able to serve God in truth.

According to the Jewish mystics, one of the main objectives of our existence is to do good deeds and to refrain from doing evil. When we commit evil, the presence of God is banished from the world, while when enough human beings live the just life, the kingdom of God will be brought to earth. If we were deprived of the choice between good and evil, we would also be unable to do right. Perhaps God required humankind to bring such a world to fulfillment. Perhaps God is not all-powerful.

The rabbinic epigram "It is not in our power to explain either the tranquility of the wicked or the sufferings of the upright" offers another possible explanation. Perhaps what we experience as incomprehensible in our perception of the world is beyond human reason and can only be comprehended through an all-embracing view of reality.

The Taoist parable of the poor man and the horse likewise reflects the difficulty of knowing what is truly good and truly evil. A man and his son owned a horse. One day the horse was gone. When his friends came to commiserate over the disappearance, the man asked them how they could know that what happened was an unfortunate event. Later, when the horse returned, bringing with it a whole flock of wild horses, the man's friends congratulated him on his good luck. Once again, the man countered with a question: "How can you know that this was my good fortune?" When his son began to break in the wild horses, he fell and broke his leg, and the man's friends returned to sympathize with him about this negative turn. Once again, he asked them how they could know this was a bad thing. Soon a war broke out, and the man's lame son was exempted from military service and able to stay safely at home.

Many religious traditions assert that God created the universe and all its laws, after which the laws have gone on working and laid the foundations for development, including the coming into being of the human race. In this view, God paved the way and is ubiquitous in the creation. But perhaps controlling evil is not part of God's "remit." Perhaps God simply created a point of departure, after which it is up to humankind to reign over both good and evil.

### Is God created by humankind to meet our own needs?

Another argument against the existence of God is found in the notion that religion and God were simply created by humankind to fulfill basic human needs. Death, the absence of meaning, loneliness, insecurity, and suffering are aspects of life that are often difficult for us to accept. Religion offers answers to almost all the difficult questions life poses, thus fulfilling our deepest desires. Those who do not believe in the existence of God would argue that the various religions do not reveal and explain truths about God, but have created a concept of God/gods in order to resolve difficult questions in life. Let us look at some of the ways that the image of the divine meets basic human needs.

*Death.* People are frightened of death for many reasons. Perhaps we fear disappearing, of no longer being with loved ones, no longer being able to enjoy the good sides of life. Religion offers a solution: eternal life, perhaps in a different form, but still forever. Each religion has its own way of describing the continuation of existence, but they all utilize the theme that some part of us will go on living after death. This may be a comforting thought since it counteracts the sense of vulnerability that may accompany the awareness of death.

*The absence of meaning in life.* Today, many people live with the feeling that life has no meaning, no point. Religion tells us this is not the case, that there is a higher aim to life. Although the ultimate context may be shrouded in mystery, there are several themes, including the idea that good deeds, wisdom, love, and right-thinking will, in the long term, lead to a more meaningful existence at a higher level, both for the individual and for all of humanity.

*Loneliness and insecurity.* Even with friends and families around them, people may feel fundamentally alone and insecure. At times, for instance after the loss of a loved one, these feelings may overpower us. Religion can offer compensation in the form of a personal God, experienced as omnipresent. Religion can also provide us with a sense of community with the world around us, a feeling of being safe and secure in that which is larger than humankind.

*Suffering.* People suffer as they grapple with the evil aspects of life. Illness, starvation, poverty, and loneliness are only a few of the many sufferings that afflict humankind. Religion offers explanations for suffering, infusing the concept with significance.

*Social structure.* Religion gives life a social structure, common moral values, and a sense of community.

Clearly, religions do offer significant answers to many of the fundamental questions of human life, as well as comfort in the midst of suffering. The question remains, however, whether God provided religions as a way of relating to humankind, or we created the idea of a relational God in order to meet our own needs.

### Why does God not appear from behind the veils?

If there is a deity, why doesn't God make a clear statement or a public appearance, so as to be acknowledged by all? Why are not all human beings born with the knowledge of the existence of God? If God appeared in a way that made it impossible to deny, this would, of course, be an incontrovertible argument for religion.

Correspondingly, we may ask ourselves why God does not state clearly what is expected of us and why. Why should we have to seek this knowledge and guess what we were meant to make of our lives? If there were an explicit platform, there would be no doubt as to the aim and point of living. The question can, of course, be reversed. We can just as well ask why we have been endowed at all with instruments and methods for exploring the divine.

The Upanishads have a theoretical explanation for why God is not revealed: "The gods love secrecy and cannot bear the literal." Some would also claim that God has already been made known to us, but we do not always see or believe the revelation. Another thought is that the search for the divine is, in itself, precisely the ultimate meaning of the search itself, and that in our attempts to comprehend a God who is beyond human understanding we have the opportunity to grow and develop.

Of course we may tell ourselves that, by definition, God is all that we are unable to experience through our senses and our consciousness. Thus, if the divinity were revealed from out of the mist it would be instantly transformed into the tangible and lose its concealed, mysterious nature. Religion and belief would be converted to fact.

Another explanation for the inaccessibility of God is that because God does not exist there is nothing to be revealed. None of the claims of the great religions as to the existence of a mystical or supernatural reality have been validated. Millennia have passed, but no evidence has been put forward to prove the existence of God, or of a system of punishment and reward for our deeds, or of a life after death.

### If God exists, why are there so many differences among religions?

Both those who believe in the existence of God and those who do not must acknowledge that there are fundamental differences among the religions of the world. If we analyze the external forms of expression of the great religions, their rites, traditions, narratives, laws, and social systems, we quickly discover that there seems to be more that separates than unites them. Some of these differences include:

+ the way they describe what happens to us after death;
+ their traditions and rites/rituals;

+ their creation myths and stories of how humankind came to be;
+ the way they describe the meaning of life and the future of humanity;
+ the way they describe a personal god;
+ the extent to which they perceive God as active.

Every religion has developed within a culture, and the external forms of a religious system reflect the reality of this culture. Certain symbols and myths function better in given contexts, and so each religion has developed its own way of describing the indescribable. However, none of this is enough to explain all the evident contradictions among religions. These differences are seen by many as a serious argument against the existence of God, since they call into question the truth of the descriptions of God put forward by the various religions.

One of the fundamental questions has to do with the spiritual experience of contact with a superior truth, which we have referred to as the concealed God. There are many common denominators among religions when it comes to this experience, but there are also differences. Take, for instance, the experience of unity with the divine. Some mystical traditions claim that the ultimate experience is total unification with the divine. Others describe this experience as an encounter with the divine, but in this experience the independence of the individual is never abolished.

Another difference is found in examining *what* the mystic encounters. Monotheistic religions refer consistently to the term "God," while other designations, such as "the Absolute," "the soul of the universe," and "nirvana" are used by Eastern religions.

Of course, one fundamental problem is that we are discussing a subject without clearly accepted definitions. We may use any words we choose, or no words at all, to describe the indescribable. Another problem is that religions have been built up on the basis of different languages, which may result in misinterpretation of descriptions in translation. A third difficulty is that the different religions have arisen in different intellectual environments. This may make it difficult for a person who has been brought up in one faith to be fully capable of understanding other belief systems. There are also geographical differences as well as differences arising over time, the result of which may be that the language adapted to one period no longer appears "alive" to future generations.

Thus although many mystics use similar words to describe the indescribable, we cannot be certain that the religious of different faiths really
share the same experience. In fact, very different experiences of God may
be clothed in similarly vague language, which is vague by necessity. The
fact that different religions all assert the indescribability of the divine is
not proof that they are discussing the same ineffable experience.

The question can also be reversed, so as to ask whether there may be a
natural explanation of the differences in the ways the concealed God is
described. It is possible that a desire on the part of religious mystics not
to find themselves in conflict with the dominant religion and culture in
their areas is one such explanation. That would mean, for instance, that
Jewish and Christian mystics adapted their descriptions of the concealed
God to a language that would not place them in opposition with the more
traditional practitioners of their religions. Otherwise, if a Jew were to
claim that there is a divine reality superior to the "one God," this might be
perceived as idolatry or polytheism, which would be in violation of the
first commandment. Similarly, if a Christian were to claim that Jesus was
not unique as a divine human being, this would also be in violation of
established dogma.

Meister Eckhart approached this problem in a special way by com-
menting on the words of Augustine of Hippo, who said that a human
being is that which he or she loves:

> If he loves a stone, he is a stone; if he loves a man, he is a man;
> if he loves God—I dare not say more, for if I said that he would
> then be God, ye might stone me.

It is precisely the indescribable nature of the experience of the divine
that can make it both natural and safe to use the symbols of one's own
religion and culture when writing about the great mystery.

The Sufi poet Rumi provides another explanation of the differences
between mystical experiences in the following narrative: Some people were
taken into a dark room where there was an elephant. They made their way
over to the creature, touched it, and then drew different conclusions about
what they found. One felt its leg and said it must be a pillar. Another felt
its back and said it must be an enormous throne. A third felt its ear and
declared it to be a surprisingly large fan. In this way, people who are

searching, but from different perspectives, may experience that which is basically the same reality in very different ways.[17] There is a fundamental distinction between what reality is actually like and how we perceive it.

Another question is how a mystical experience can be channeled if there is no religious form for describing it. Without the norms and ethical framework of established religion, mystical experience may be expressed in ways that manifest destructive powers, both for individuals, groups, and entire societies. History bears witness to individuals in cults and other groups who have broken with established religions to wander "the path of truth," and in doing so have caused severe damage to themselves and the world around them. Similarly, political forces may claim a "divine calling" as a justification for their horrendous crimes. This is one reason why religions both accentuate the dangers associated with taking the route of mysticism in the absence of a true spiritual leader and warn against false prophets.

A related argument against the existence of the divine likewise has to do with differences among religions: religious intolerance. Various religions profess their own way as the only true route to God. Such intolerance may express itself both toward other religions and toward different schools within the same religion. Lack of respect for other religions sometimes also takes expression in violence. Jonathan Swift, a clergyman in addition to being an author, said this: "We have just enough religion to make us hate, but not enough to make us love one another."

When those who invoke the existence of a God also assert that their particular faith gives them the right to abuse the practitioners of other schools of religion, it is tempting to conclude that the true aim of religious systems is actually far from seeking the divine. Naturally, one can object that religious intolerance has nothing to do with divinity, but is merely an expression of human frailty and shortcomings. However, it is difficult to argue on the basis of only certain aspects of religion being "true." If that were so, how could we ever be certain of which aspects actually are the true ones?

Of course no religion will ever be able to provide us with the entire truth about the divine. All religion can do is to serve as an aid to us in our search—and this search may occupy our entire lifetime. Practition-

17. This is a theme that appears with variations in other cultures as well. The earliest written account claims that the story was told by Buddha (Udana 6:4).

ers of different religions can, in this respect, share a rewarding sense of community, while those who claim to have found the whole truth may not even have begun to search in earnest.

## SOME ARGUMENTS
## IN FAVOR OF THE EXISTENCE OF GOD
### *The miracle of creation reveals God*

One argument in favor of the existence of God has to do with the mysteries inherent in the amazingly complex universe in which we live. As we saw in the section on God and science, incredible complexity and diversity are necessary for the existence of all life. Although science has been able to provide increasingly accurate descriptions of the laws of nature and the events that gave rise to the universe and to life, and although many of our questions may be answered, it is possible that others will never be answered fully. These unanswered questions can lead people to conclude that there must be a spiritual reality, a moving force that could be called God.

Just when we think we have found the answer to a particular question, we discover another, and then another. The discovery of chemical and biological processes controlled by predetermined principles has provided us with a partial explanation to the origins of life. But where did these principles come from? The universe operates in accordance with the laws of physics. But why did these particular laws come into existence, rather than others that would have made it impossible for the world to arise at all? More and more details about how the world came into being have become available to us. But how did the process begin? And beyond each and every one of these questions, there is a more fundamental question: "Why?" Why were the universe and all life created? Why did humankind, with the ability to ask questions about its own existence, come into being?

Accepting a spiritual reality and a divine explanation underpinning reason and common sense may be one way of relating to these unsolved riddles about our own existence, the complexity of nature, or the creation of the universe. All these phenomena may be regarded as arguments for the existence of a reality and a truth beyond that which science can explain today.

## Morals and ethics reflects the divine

Although human beings sometimes commit evil deeds, most of what we do is good. The vast majority of human beings are driven by an internal sense of right and a clear feeling for what actions are reprehensible. Various alternative explanations for why humankind was endowed with a sense of morals and ethics have been discussed earlier. The explanation put forward by religion is that there is a "natural law of ethics." In monotheism this is intimately related to the divine.

It has been asserted that if there were no divinity, we would have to invent God, because otherwise human society would decompose morally. Whether or not there was a God, human beings would require, for their sheer survival, laws and norms based on ethical principles. This may, in its turn, be put forward as an argument against the belief that the divine is the provider of an ethical foundation.

## Emotional experiences of God

Throughout history, seekers of different religions have borne testimony to experiencing the God of concealed reality, and to the encounter with supreme love, goodness, and wisdom as the marks of the divine. Is it, then, truly God these seekers experience? The Jewish philosopher Martin Buber (1878–1965) describes his own personal mystical experiences, referring to them as inward-turning experiences of the self. The Kabbalah also contains descriptions of mystics encountering their own selves.

Thus the question as to whether the testimony of human spiritual seekers may be regarded as proof of the existence of the divine is an open one.

## The problem in disproving God

An atheist can be defined as a person who denies or disbelieves the existence of a supreme being or beings.[18] The hypothesis of a concealed God contains the problem that, by definition, the atheist does not know what he or she is denying. Paradoxically, because a hidden God can only be

18. *Webster's Unabridged,* 3rd edition. In *The Encyclopedia of Religion,* atheism is defined as "the denial that there is any 'god' no matter in what sense god is defined." The term atheism is sometimes used to describe *the belief* that there is no God. Just as religious individuals may assert that their creed is, fundamentally, knowledge, atheists may claim an inner conviction that God does not exist.

experienced but never described, an atheist would have to have had such an experience prior to being able to deny the existence of God.

Atheists may claim that one cannot believe in a God for the existence of whom there is no proof. Of course, religion cannot cope with this problem because, by definition, a concealed God cannot be proven. The absence of evidence for something, however, does not automatically lead to the reverse conclusion—that is, the absence of evidence is not proof of the non-existence of that very thing. This would be just as wrong as demanding that a human being who has not had an experience of the divine unconditionally accept the existence of God.

Being convinced that there is no God on the basis of what we can experience with our five senses and our intellect is not unlike what was once a general conviction that the world was flat. It, too, was founded on logical thinking and on the fact that we experience reality through our senses. So as we learn more and more from science about the complexity of the universe and nature, we become correspondingly aware of how little of reality we actually understand.

This may also be described in terms of a parable. A man was shut up in a dark room and told that there might also be a butterfly in the room. After waiting a few moments, he concluded that there could not possibly be a butterfly there: "I cannot see it, cannot hear it, cannot smell it, and cannot feel it. As none of these senses experience the butterfly, it does not exist." Let us now make things slightly more difficult for this man by assuming that he had never seen or heard of butterflies. Although he had reason to suspect that there may be something in the room, he had no idea of what it was, because he possessed no knowledge of the object.

A concealed God cannot be readily accessible to our senses and many of us have no idea what we would be expected to encounter in a meeting with the divine. A skeptic might conclude that *in all probability* the butterfly, or God, does not exist. Suddenly, he would no longer be an atheist, but he would have been transformed into an agnostic.

### The similarities among religions indicate an ultimate reality

All the major religions maintain that there is some kind of metaphysical reality. Although in some respects they each describe it differently, there are also many similarities. As we have seen earlier, they all have similar moral/ethical world views, notions of life after death, rites, traditions, myths, and descriptions of a concealed God. An Indian folk song formulates the idea of the divine shared by the great religions as follows:

Into the bosom of the one great sea
Flow streams that come from hills on every side,
Their names are various as their springs,
And thus in every land do men bow down
To one great God, though known by many names.

For some, these similarities among religions point to a shared revelation of a single divine reality that is simply called by different names and are thus regarded as an argument in favor of the existence of God.

## DOES GOD EXIST?

As always, this debate leaves us in uncertainty. Because it is a discussion about something that defies description, there is no alternative. All assertions of full knowledge of the divine appear as wrongly formulated as all claims that there cannot possibly be a God. The demand that we should have blind faith in God seems as unreasonable as the declaration that rational thinking can provide us with all the answers. Thus once again we must conclude that it is up to every individual to ask the question and then, with the aid of methods of his or her own choosing, search for the answer.

## ∾ 15

# The Search for a Concealed God

*"But," the* LORD *said, "you cannot see my face; for no one shall see me and live."*

—Exodus 33:20

AROUND THE INNERMOST TRUTHS of every religion is woven a fabric of rites, traditions, myths, ethical and moral norms, social functions, and more. These aspects have often come to dominate religions, but this may not always have been the case. Several religions describe how, in the distant past, humankind lived in direct contact with the spiritual (divine), without need of religious rites and traditions. The biblical narrative of Adam and Eve encountering God face to face in the Garden of Eden may be interpreted as a description of a phase in which people lived in simple unity with the divine. When human beings tasted the fruit of the tree of knowledge, taking the symbolic step from the consciousness of the animals to a higher level of thinking, the immediacy of contact with God was lost, and humankind was exiled from paradise.

At that stage structured religion may have been unnecessary, in that every individual had a given relation to the divine. In accordance with this theory, humankind was eventually torn out of this undisturbed experience of the divine and had to seek what could then only be intimated. It was in relation to this search that the various religions sprang up.

Most religions describe methods people can use in their search for an experience of that which is concealed. These methods often share the theme of the necessity to seek God within. According to this thought, we do not need to travel anywhere to find God; we need not seek the divine in heaven or in unknown worlds. God is to be sought in the deepest recesses of human consciousness, as described in a poem by the Sufi poet Jalaluddin Rumi:

I am not hidden in what is high or low
Nor in the earth nor skies nor throne.
This is certainty, O Beloved:
I am hidden in the heart of the faithful.
If you seek me, seek in these hearts.

At times book learning is even seen as an obstacle to the search for the divine. For instance, take this Sufi tale of a learned man seeking the highest insight. In his search for a master, he is robbed of all his books and forced to abandon learning as a path to salvation. After years of inner search, and eventually finding the highest truth, he gradually becomes aware that the loss of his books was a precondition for finding the true way. (This view of the value of books is not, however, a generalized one.)

We cannot find God in another person. Others can only help guide us. Neither should we seek God in history, which can merely give us experience. According to religions, God can never be found "there." "Here and now" are the place and time to search, turning our gazes inward and seeking the divine there. Religions assert that an individual who tirelessly and honestly seeks in this way will find wondrous things along the journey and at its goal.

In a tale shared by many cultures with only slight variations, a man dreamed one night that he had to leave for a far away city where he was supposed to dig for treasure under the city wall. When he woke up, he decided to embark on the long journey to that city to seek his fortune. Time passed in the distant city and one night a guard addressed him, asking why he was spending so much time searching around the wall. When he told the guard about his dream, the guard laughed and retorted that he, too, had had a dream, in which he had been instructed to go to the man's hometown and seek his fortune in the man's hearth. The guard advised the man to stop following his dreams and return home. The man thanked him, did so, and found the treasure, not unexpectedly, in his own hearth.

The point of this story is that the "treasure" is inside each and every one of us. We do not need to seek our fortune, peace, or the divine elsewhere. All we seek is already right there, inside us. However, the story also has it that we may sometimes need to make a journey and seek elsewhere in order to realize that inside ourselves is the only place we can find what is truly important. The story has another level as well, pointing out that our subconscious, our dreams, can express the guidance we need in our search for the divine. If we listen to our inner voice, our chance of arriving at the ultimate goal may increase.

What, then, makes a human being decide to seek the divine? That search bears little similarity to a treasure hunt, since we are not searching for material assets. Neither is it like searching for power and influence. When we seek these things, we know what feeling we are trying to achieve. The search for the divine is the search for something unknown, and even more than unknown, indescribable.

Various factors may motivate a person in this process of inward seeking. Sometimes the decision is rooted in relatively brief experiences of a spiritual nature that inspire the person to choose the long path to insight. Sometimes these are experiences from childhood or adolescence that may have dissipated with the coming of adulthood. At other times they are experiences related to periods when life inflicts pain upon us. Job experiences the divine after a long period of grief and despair, and he says: "I had heard of you by the hearing of the ear, but now my eye sees you" (Job 42:5).

Others may choose to place their confidence in the tales and descriptions they have heard from people who have experienced the indescribable truth. Perhaps, indeed, humankind was created to seek knowledge beyond that which is readily comprehensible.

What are the common principles for the inner search for that which is concealed? The methods may vary, but religious traditions have a number of recurrent themes.

## MEDITATION, CONTEMPLATION, AND PRAYER

The Book of Psalms says: "Be still, and know that I am God!" (46:10). The same theme, the necessity of inner silence and peace in order to reach the highest knowledge, can be found in all the major religions. We must quiet the constant flow of impressions and the din of our thoughts because they pose obstacles to contact with inner reality. We cannot see the reflection of the sun in a choppy sea, but only in waters that are entirely still, without a ripple on the surface. Similarly, we cannot find the reflection of the divine in a consciousness agitated with feelings, thoughts, and sensory impressions.

The various techniques for achieving this peace of mind are often referred to in religion as contemplation, meditation, or prayer. One frequent method is to concentrate our awareness first on one isolated thought, and then gradually to empty it altogether. For instance, concentration can first be focused on particular words and sentences, through images or awareness of breathing. Finally, when thoughts fade entirely, we can experience a different, inner reality. From that point, the individual can move on to deeper and deeper insights.

Body posture is central to many kinds of meditation, prayer, and contemplation. Our inner search is dependent on having our outer selves, our bodies, in as positive a position as possible. The lotus position, sitting with legs crossed and back erect, is one such ideal pose. True masters cease to need special physical positions. They are said to be able to experience the proximity of the divine in everything they do.

## LIVING IN THE PRESENT

A woman asked Buddha how to meditate, and he answered that she could meditate by being perfectly attentive to her every movement as she pulled water up from the well. Thus he highlighted the importance of living in the moment, instead of in memories of the past or plans for the future.

Jesus highlighted the importance of living in the present when he said: "So do not worry about tomorrow, for tomorrow will bring worries of its own" (Matthew 6:34). A Sufi proverb puts it similarly: "Do not regret the past and do not worry about the future." There is also a Buddhist parable of a man who was being chased by a tiger. He eventually found himself hanging from a cliff on a fraying vine, about to drop. At that very moment he discovered a delectable berry growing in a little crevice in the cliff. The man consumed the berry, savoring the moment and not brooding about the future.

We are taught that we should live our lives in the present. By focusing our consciousness on this moment and nothing else, we can make everything we do a kind of meditation, be it washing the dishes or tying our shoes. The Jewish philosopher Maimonides (1135–1204) described ordinary human beings as reaching a stage of consciousness higher than that of the prophets, nearly as high as that of Moses, when "our hearts may be constantly close to God, but our bodies are in the community of humankind."

## WITH AN OPEN HEART

Religions often tell us that our inner search must be conducted with great fixity of purpose, while we must also constantly abstain from individual expectation and anticipation of what we will find. As a rule, we are told, all our traditional conceptions, linguistic and intellectual alike, only pose obstacles along the path to insight. God and mystical reality are consistently described as "entirely different" from what we normally experience through consciousness. A Buddhist expression puts it dramatically: "If you meet Buddha on the road, strike him dead." In order to reach insight we must give up all preconceived notions. In line with this idea, many monotheistic mystics hold that thinking about what God actually "is" may prevent us from knowing. The Christian theologian Gregory of Nyssa (334–394) put it like this: "Every concept of God is a mere simulacrum, a false likeness, an idol: it could not reveal God himself." Thus it is clear that in our search for God we must combine determination with humility and an open heart, accepting that although this inward search may entice the highest insight to reveal itself, it can never force it into visibility.

In fact, perhaps the immediate aim should not be to achieve higher and higher insight or to come closer to God, but simply to live our lives righteously and to learn as this journey progresses. If we are able to leave it at that, the rest may come, not as part of a focused striving for the divine, but as a consequence of our endeavor to do what is right. When we peer into the darkness and glimpse something barely distinguishable we tend to find that we see it more clearly if we fix our gaze not upon it but alongside it.

## RENOUNCING THE EGO

*The true value of a human being is determined primarily by the measure and the sense in which he has attained liberation from the self.*
—Albert Einstein

Many mystical traditions hold that to complete the journey we must abandon our ego, our personality: "Whoever is full of himself has no room for God." As long as we cling to the illusion of the great significance of the self, seeing everything in relation to our own personalities, we will remain cut off from the deepest truths. As long as we strive for personal success, honor, and fame, we will also be preventing ourselves from completing the journey. According to the *Tao Te Ching:* "Rather than glitter like jade He must stand like stone."

In some religions, such as Buddhism, this renunciation of personality is based on the laboriously gained insight that the ego is nothing but a transient construction. In Islam, the abandonment is based more on subservience to that which is infinitely greater than the self.

The biblical expression "The fear of [respect for] the Lord is the beginning of wisdom" (Psalm 111:10) reminds us that the insight, gained through humility, of our own miniscule size in relation to God is what enables us to understand the great truths. Jewish mysticism, like Confucianism, emphasizes the importance of humility, but often without stressing the need to renounce the self. Jewish mysticism does, however, occasionally affirm that "when we wholly and fully abandon the self, we are empty. Being empty, we also become vessels for the higher forms of light in the world."

"Mystical death" is a concept shared by various traditions of mysticism, and refers to the necessity of allowing our old self to perish so that we can be in contact with the divine. One example may be found in the words of Paul: "Therefore we have been buried with him by baptism into death, so that, just as Christ was raised from the dead by the glory of the Father, so we too might walk in newness of life" (Romans 6:4). Another is a Sufi saying: "God should make thee die to thyself and should make thee live in him." Taoism, too, asserts that during our lives we must "die in order to live," and these words from the Hebrew scriptures may reflect a similar thought: "I will remove from your body the heart of stone and give you a heart of flesh" (Ezekiel 36:26).

The mystics tell us that renunciation of the ego, such a difficult task for us Western individualists, will lead to the experience of being at one with all things and offer us insight and joy far deeper than that which we can find in asserting our selves.

## HOW WE LIVE OUR LIVES

Consideration for our fellow human beings is a recurrent theme in all religions, encompassing love, kindness, charity, compassion, humility, forgiveness, thoughtfulness, and refraining from harming or inflicting hurt upon others. The ethical rules and laws of religions have all developed on the basis of these principles.

The religions also tell us that these qualities will follow automatically from achieving the highest insight about God. Before we possess it, we must learn to live righteously. Although we may initially comply with ethical principles for superficial reasons, our inner moral system will gradually develop as a result of righteous living. Today we may be kind and compassionate to others because we have been told to be, but gradually consideration and love for our fellow human beings will become a drive emanating from within.

Another frequent theme is that we may experience the divine in the encounter with a fellow human being. By learning to understand, respect, and see others, we will also come closer to the divine. Thus religions tell us that a life lived in respect and love for our fellow human beings may have a dimension beyond the ethical and moral.

According to many religions, a just life is an absolute prerequisite for gaining the ultimate insight and closeness to the divine. If we have not internalized a moral code, we may devote endless amounts of time to prayer, meditation, and contemplation to no avail. We may dutifully observe all the rituals and traditions, but they will remain incomplete until we also live righteously.

## SOLITUDE AND ISOLATION

*He who is unable to live in society, or who has no need because he is sufficient for himself, must be either a beast or a god.*

—Aristotle

Despite our fundamental human need for life in community, many religions hold that a person should spend time in solitude as part of the search for the divine. Jesus, Muhammad, and Buddha all withdrew into isolation at times before coming forward as heralds of their messages and these periods gave them great insight. The ultimate type of retreat may be found in the ideal of the hermit and some aspects of monasticism. Those who devote themselves to these ways of life also devote all their time to the search for God.

Religions also emphasize the necessity of self-denial. We should understand that material welfare may even be an obstacle on the path to insight. These thoughts take their most extreme form in the ideal of asceticism, the forsaking of both worldly things and worldly pleasures.

Although few people are considered suited to spending a lifetime in isolation (or would wish to), many religions assert that if a person desires to find God, some periods of time should be spent in solitude. By taking the opportunity to withdraw from the madding crowd, we also have a chance to quiet our thoughts and listen for the voice that can only be discerned as a whisper in utter silence.

## FINDING A SPIRITUAL GUIDE

According to most traditions, we need a spiritual guide to help us to the ultimate insights. We may begin our search alone, but as a rule we will require a mentor along the way. Who shall we then appoint to this position? One possibility is a representative of a religious community—a clergyperson, an imam, a rabbi, a Buddhist monk, or a Hindu guru; another is a wise believer without official authority. There are also wise, enlightened men and women outside the institutions of religion. We simply need to find them.

How can we know when a person is a true spiritual leader rather than a "false prophet"? Some principles that may guide us in our search for a truly spiritual individual may include:

+ A spiritual guide would accept other religions and creeds, as long as these are not evil. It might be unadvisable to select a practitioner of religion who declares that his or her own religion is the only true religion, the only true path to God.
+ A spiritual guide would not flaunt him- or herself.
+ A spiritual guide would favor nonviolence, even for purposes of disseminating "the truth."
+ A spiritual guide would possess personal spiritual experience.
+ A spiritual guide would be humble, loving, peaceful, kind, ethically sound, and forgiving.

It should be clear from the above that it is not an easy task to find a spiritual advisor. It can take years, and a number of alternatives are likely to be rejected before the final choice is made.

## FINDING OUR OWN WAY

A wise Jewish man was once asked why he did not live in the same way as his teacher. He answered that he followed him in every way, and "as he once left *his* teacher, I have left him."

Buddha spoke tirelessly of the importance of finding one's own way. He held that, in this respect, the institutions of religion could do more harm than good. This accentuation of the importance of finding one's own way may seem paradoxical considering the importance religions attach to the need for spiritual guidance. The explanation lies in the fact that the search itself must always finally be a personal journey, in relation to which others may only indicate the direction to travel. In the end, each of us must choose our own way. There is nothing barring a human being from the divine, and for that very reason the journey is ultimately each person's own decision and responsibility.

## DOUBT AND QUESTIONING ARE PERMITTED

Religions that not only allow us to doubt but even encourage skepticism include Judaism, Buddhism, and Hinduism. When, in his despair, Job questions the justice and the decisions of God: "But I would speak to the Almighty, and I desire to argue my case with God" (Job 13:3), God clearly accepts Job's right to doubt. Perhaps a God we are not allowed to doubt will eventually appear lifeless to us, while a God we may doubt can remain full of life.

In Christianity we find the expression "the dark night of the soul," referring to a period in which a person may feel cut off from God. The path to greater nearness to the divine may sometimes be blocked with doubts when the sense of spirituality vanishes. Because we human beings have a peculiar ability to reassess emotional experiences once they are behind us, this absence of faith may lead an individual to abandon the search. One unfortunate consequence may be that the person continues to claim adherence to a faith with a conviction no longer based on either reason or emotion.

Wise men say that we must not blindly accept "truths" communicated to us by others. That would be basing our faith on shaky foundations and, in turn, would put us at risk of becoming fanatics. In the words of Lama

Anagarika Govinda: "He who believes blindly in anything—be it good or bad—is not the master of it." Fanaticism is always rooted in an unconscious, inner insecurity and is the result of our efforts to battle it down by striking out at things outside ourselves. We project outside ourselves the doubt and uncertainty we refuse to allow inside.

For this reason, it is our right, perhaps even our obligation, to doubt during the course of our search for the innermost truths. Because we are searching for something that is, by all definitions, beyond our senses and all human comprehension, we will never be in possession of complete knowledge of it. No matter how much effort or faith we invest, we will ultimately have to accept that we cannot have all the answers. The Talmud tells us that "on this subject there were differences of opinion between two Palestinian sages, and there are those who say that it was a debate between two angels from Heaven." If not even the angels can be all-knowing, how can we imagine that we might?

What is important is the search itself, in humility and in the aspiration of greater understanding. Mahatma Gandhi, one of the greatest thinkers of the twentieth century, said in his autobiography: "I worship God as Truth only. I have not yet found Him, but I am seeking after Him. I am prepared to sacrifice the things dearest to me in pursuit of this quest." Even if we come to understand things better and gain greater insight, in the final analysis the great mystery remains and, according to the scholars, we may only approach it with the utmost humility and wonder. This is how things were meant to be. Therefore, any person who claims to possess the ultimate truth has not at all found wisdom but, in the end, only lost his way.

## DIVINE GRACE

According to some traditions of mysticism, the personal search can only take us to a certain point and no further. There, we must wait for the ultimate experience to reveal itself. This experience is referred to variously as "enlightenment," "insight," "wisdom," and "awareness of God." In monotheistic religions, these truths come to us by what is known as "the grace of God." Our inner search may pave the way, but we cannot take the last steps purposefully. They will come to us when we are ready.

## THE LONG PATH

Religions agree that the inner search is a long journey toward the final goal, a search that may last for many years. Some even claim that it may last for many lifetimes. Although we may occasionally experience a sense of the divine along the way, we will still be mercilessly and repeatedly drawn back to our old way of living and thinking, to doubt and uncertainty. We may have the feeling that, in spite of transient progress, we return to square one. We may believe that we have reached our goal, only to find that we were wrong. In such a situation, grave errors may be made. Instead of continuing the search, we may allow fanaticism and fundamentalism to rule us, believing that we have accomplished the journey. Having only achieved false wisdom, built on shifting sand, we refuse to let anyone deprive us of it. This state may be experienced both by individuals and by sects. Sometimes it may even happen to whole religions. The scholars remind us that we must accept that the path is inevitably a long one.

There is a Buddhist tale about a young man who wished to learn the art of fencing from a renowned master. He inquired of the master how long it would take, and was told ten years. Finding this far too long, he asked whether he might not accelerate the process with extra practice. The master's answer was that, in that case, it could well take him thirty years. Believing himself to have been misunderstood, the young man explained that he was in a great hurry to master the art as quickly as possible. This time the master's answer was that with that attitude seventy years might suffice for him to learn to fence.

We must fully accept that the inner search will take time and that there are no direct routes. We must wander the spiritual path patiently, not constantly on the lookout for results, which will come when we least expect them. However, there is no reason to despair over the fact that the journey is long. Wise men assure us that there are "rewards" along the way in the form of greater inner peace, wisdom, happiness, and an increased ability to help our fellow human beings. The journey is also a goal in itself.

## MANY WAYS TO THE DIVINE

There are many paths to the highest knowledge. A person who is not bound to a given creed has many opportunities to seek the divine. A person who feels more bound to the religion he or she was brought up in has opportunities within it. It is important to locate those people who set great store by the search for the divine, and who also have the ability to teach. This will mean—undoubtedly to the relief of some—that there is no need to abandon a religion with which one feels a strong affinity. Thus the answer offered here to the question, "Which way shall I choose?" is, "Whichever way feels right." The Jewish philosopher Martin Buber put it very well: "Everyone should carefully observe what way his heart draws him to, and then choose this way with all his strength."

## ⌒ 16

## *What Is God?*

Seekers from different religious traditions describe similar means of achieving the experience of an indescribable supreme reality, sometimes referred to as God, sometimes in other terms. Is the same experience shared by different religious seekers, or does the innermost truth vary from one religion to another? Is there one God, are there many gods, or are there none? One way of tackling this question might be to do what scientists do when they find that the results of a series of experiments are contradictory. After due consideration, they choose among the following explanations:

+ The hypothesis being investigated in the experiments was erroneous. In this case, the fact that searches carried out in different religious traditions while using similar methods produced different end results implies that the hypothesis that there is a God is invalid.
+ Only some of the scientific experiments gave the correct results, while all the others failed to do so. This would mean, when applied to religion, that only certain religions have "done things right" and found the real God. All the others have failed to achieve contact with the divine, and consequently they describe false gods and untruths.
+ The experiments gave different results, all of which are correct. This hypothesis would imply that there are many gods.
+ The experiments were all performed correctly but the results were interpreted differently. This would mean that the different religions describe the same and only God, but in somewhat different ways.

The different religions appear to agree, in many respects, about what the divine represents. This may mean that the religious "experiments" produced the same results and that the discrepancies only arose when attempting to explain them. For that reason, I have kept to the hypothesis that people who seek in similar ways also ultimately have similar experiences and then interpret and describe them in words that are effective in their particular cultural contexts. This hypothesis implies that if there is a concealed God, the different religions have found this common divine essence.

In what respects do the religions appear to agree? What common conclusions have the different seekers drawn with regard to a divine power beyond words? We concluded above that, by definition, God is completely indescribable, and this makes a discussion of what the divine actually is a paradoxical one. If the concealed God exists and has intentions with regard to us, those intentions should also, by definition, be beyond our ability to comprehend. And yet mystics of various religions try time and again to describe the indescribable. If we consider their endeavors to be attempts to describe how the indescribable God is reflected in reality as we know it, they may offer us at least partial answers to these extraordinarily complex questions.

## GOD WITHIN

*The Self is hidden in the lotus of the heart. Those who see themselves in all creatures go day by day into the world of Brahman hidden in the heart.*
—The Upanishads

According to the mystical traditions of religions, God is in every human being. Judaism describes this aspect of God as neshama. Christianity calls it the Holy Spirit, for which there is room in the soul of every human being. The Sufis speak of Allah as being in everything and thus also in human beings. In Hinduism, the divine aspect of the human being is known as Atman, while in Buddhism we find the descriptions of "nirvana element" or "Buddha nature." This omnipresent divine aspect of humankind is closely related to love, wisdom, and compassion with all living things.

Many religions assert that some people live so completely in awareness of this divine aspect of human nature that they become "divine beings" themselves, or are "animated by the divine spirit." Traditional Christianity has it that this has only fully happened once, in the person of Jesus from Nazareth, who expressed his unity with the divine when he said, "The Father and I are one" (John 22:10). It should also be noted, however, that Augustine spoke of God as being more inherent in all beings in creation than they are in themselves. And in Christian mysticism we sometimes encounter the idea that every human being has the potential to become (and basically is) divine.

In its strict monotheism, Judaism has always cast a stern eye toward those who have claimed to possess divinity. The Book of Psalms does say, "You are gods, children of the Most High, all of you" (82:6), but the verse is open to interpretation. So, for Jews who experience total unity with the divine, the only even remote possibility has been the belief that the Messiah, a human being with "divine powers" (yet still not a "god") will appear on earth. Hence it is not surprising to find people within Jewish mysticism time and again claiming to be the Messiah, with followers perfectly prepared to accept this idea.

Hinduism, with its tolerant view of diversity in relation to divinities, has had many people posing as and being regarded as incarnations of gods. Hindu scripture contains expressions such as "I am He," interpreted to mean that we are all basically divine or, in the words of Swami Nikhilananda: "In the deepest, truest sense, humankind is God." However, few ordinary mortals are actually fortunate enough to experience this fully.

In Buddhism, the human ideal is to reach the ultimate truth, and thus to become one with nirvana, although this does not mean that nirvana is usually separate from us. On the contrary, nirvana is always present inside us, although we may not be aware of it. Dilgo Khyentse Rinpoche says, "When the nature of mind is recognized, it is called nirvana." The infinite and inexpressible qualities of primordial wisdom, "the true nirvana," are inherent in our mind. Those who obtain this state are considered holy and may be prayed to in a way other religions reserve for the divine.


## REAL REALITY AND ITS UNITY

*To see a World in a grain of sand,*
*And a Heaven in a wild flower,*
*Hold Infinity in the palm of your hand,*
*And Eternity in an hour.*
　　　　　　　　　　　　—William Blake

Life, the world, and our universe are more than that which we can experience with our five senses. All we know about reality in the sensory world are simply those aspects that, like the tip of the iceberg, can be discerned at the surface of the water. Our experience of reality is not an illusion, but can, instead, be described as a shadow image. With our senses and our intellect, we attempt to understand and describe that which is infinitely more complex than we can even imagine.

In "real reality" there are truths we have been unable to measure with scientific instruments or to understand through logic, reason, and thought. When religion speaks of "future worlds," we may be misled into thinking of other worlds, whereas the interpretation of the expression should perhaps rather be this world, but experienced truly. As the apocryphal Gospel According to Thomas puts it:

His disciples said to him, "When will the kingdom come?" Jesus said, "It will not come by waiting for it. It will not be a matter of saying 'here it is' or 'there it is.' Rather, the kingdom of the father is spread out upon the earth, and men do not see it." (Thomas 113)

In this reality, everything is part of one unified fabric that resists every attempt at description. Buddha said: "In essence, things are not two but one." Similarly, the Jewish mystical book the Zohar says: "If one contemplates the things in mystical meditation, everything is revealed as one." When people experience mystical insight, they find that the words "I," "it," "us," and "them" lose their relevance, that fundamentally everything is one. In the words of the Taoist master Zhuang Zi: "The cosmos and I were born together, the ten thousand things and I are one."

This experience gives the monotheistic concept a particular meaning. Not only is there only one God because there are no others, but there is only one God because there is only one reality and everything in this reality is God.

It is said that the nature of our thoughts and their constant dynamism prevent us from experiencing this unity and the omnipresence of God. Our consciousness exists in the fragmented world, like vessels once whole and now smashed to smithereens. We are back in the cave of Plato, chained to a wall where reality can only be represented as two-dimensional shadows wavering in front of our eyes. If we are to be able to leave the cave and experience "real" reality, we will have to break the shackles of our senses, our intellect, and our ego.

## GOD AS THE BASIS OF
## AND ULTIMATE REASON FOR ALL THINGS

According to the Upanishads, Brahman is not only the principle and creator of all there is, but is also the sum totality of the universe and its phenomena. Many religions share the idea that the divine has no substance but is still the precondition and the reason for all existence. Sometimes this ultimate driving force is also experienced as immutable. Tao, for instance, is described as fixed but at the same time as the force out of which all else has arisen. Meister Eckhart said of the divinity that "for this ground is an impartible stillness, motionless in itself, and by this immobility all things are moved." Aristotle, too, spoke of the image of the "unmoved mover."

The explanation of *how* the concealed God maintains the universe is shrouded in a haze. Yet religions return, time and again, to the thought of a concealed God as the inner kernel of all things or, as the early Christian mystic Clement of Alexandria said, "God is the heart of the universe."

## THE INDESCRIBABLE GOD

According to the mystical traditions in religion, God cannot be described and will never be describable. By definition, mysticism implies that God is beyond words. The Jewish mystic Isaac Luria said of attempts to describe the indescribable:

It is impossible, because all things are interrelated. I can hardly open my mouth to speak without feeling as though the sea burst its dams and overflowed. How then shall I express what my soul has received, and how can I put it down in a book?

One particular tradition shared by many mystics is the use of negations to describe the divine. Words like "nothingness," "darkness," and "the void" are used freely about the unnamable. God is "nothing," or "darkness that shines more brightly than any light."[19] This is not meant to be interpreted as the non-existence of God, but rather as a statement that God does not exist in the same way as the things we experience through our senses. The moment we try to give the divine a designation, the entire experience vanishes. God is *completely different* from the images we create of the divine, and God cannot be compared with anything else. One of the implications of this is that God has no personal attributes. The divine, as Meister Eckhart said, is "neither the one nor the other." We cannot describe the divine. It is in the interstices between words that we may find God.

Monotheistic mystical traditions consistently choose to retain the term "God" to describe the divine who is beyond the God we find, for example, in the Bible. Other religions, such as Buddhism and Taoism, refrain from using designations such as "God" for the force inherent in all we experience as well as in that which is concealed. This may be just as well, since the word "God" has been so much used and abused. It may also be wise since it is said that in order to reach God we must abandon all words for God. Still, perhaps we should not entirely abandon a term that represents the highest ideal: the ultimate wisdom, the deepest truth, the best of the good, the most loving. Possibly the best thing to do is to retain the term in humble awareness of the fact that the designation in no way reveals anything about the qualities of its "owner."

## GOD AND TIME

Religions assert that the divine is beyond what we perceive as time, and that the concealed God is fundamentally unchangeable. This implies that God has always existed and will continue to exist for all eternity. Augustine held that time is a quality of the world created by God. The Sufi mystic Jami said, "He created the verdant fields of Time and Space and the life-giving garden of the world." This is in line with the words of the Jewish thinker Maimonides: "We hold the view that time is created." The Taoists use the term "Tao" to describe eternal reality beyond time: "It exists prior to heaven and earth and, indeed, for all eternity."

19. The word "light" is used in many religions as a designation for the divine. It is to be noted that although this light is an entirely different light than the sensory impression mediated by the eye, it can be "blinding" in intensity. Another interesting way of putting it that occurs, for example, in John of the Cross is "beam of darkness."

Some Hindu and Buddhist scholars even claim that time and space are created in our own consciousness, so that we will be able to perceive the material world. As discussed above, these thoughts run parallel to the standpoint of contemporary physics, that time came into being concomitantly with the universe.

## DOES GOD NEED HUMANKIND?

Religions are divided on the question of whether God needs humankind, or is so omnipotent as to have no real need of us. The mystical schools of Islam and Judaism are the primary ones to claim that humankind is needed to fill particular functions in creation. The special covenant that monotheism regards God as having entered into with human beings may also be interpreted as an expression of this belief.

> God said, "This is the sign of the covenant that I make between me and you and every living creature that is with you, for all future generations: I have set my bow in the clouds, and it shall be a sign of the covenant between me and the earth." (Genesis 9:12–13)

Some Sufi sources claim that God is reflected in humankind, or even that God is realized *through* humankind. However, the way in which humankind satisfies some need of God's is not made explicit. Similarly, some Christian mystics, such as Meister Eckhart, assert that God gains awareness through humankind.

Jewish mystics take the thought even further, stating that humankind is essential to the completion of the creation. In the metaphor of the vessels that shattered in conjunction with the creation of the visible universe it is said that only humankind is capable of repairing it, and when the job is done the perfect world will come into being, in accordance with God's original intentions. God needs humankind to perform this mission. Jewish mystics, too, may state that God becomes self-aware through humankind. Judaism also stresses that the human search for God is an inevitable undertaking, which we must not shirk.

Another thought sometimes appears subtly, based on the idea that God "is becoming" and that this bringing to fulfillment of the divine to some extent takes place in human consciousness. This idea, which highlights a reciprocal relationship between God and humankind, stands in contrast to the idea that God is beyond time.

Some schools of religion do not speak at all of God as needing humankind. Hinduism describes "divine play," in which the world inhabited by human beings becomes the plaything of the divine. Buddhism does not offer any explicit expression of reciprocity. Nirvana is eternal and immutable, and appears to exist for humankind rather than the other way around. Taoism sees Tao as free from any actual intention and not as existing for the well-being of humankind.

Thus there is no agreement about this issue. If God needs us, as some schools claim, it is not in a manner that we, with our limited intellect, can fully comprehend. We are part of a creation perceived as divine. Without humankind God might not be "complete." Can this be compared with losing an arm or a leg, or perhaps more suitably with the loss of a much-loved plaything? We can speculate, but only once again with the aid of symbols and descriptors with which we attempt to express a truth that ultimately cannot be put into words. However, many theological problems, including those dealing with evil, would lose their relevance if the thought of God did not contain the notion of "almighty."

## GOD IS GOOD

None of the major religions disputes the idea that God is good. All religions also state explicitly that we have been put on earth to choose the good and refrain from evil. This "natural law" of ethics implies that good deeds have positive effects extending beyond the deeds themselves, while the negative consequences of evil deeds surpass the evil of the deeds themselves. This idea is expressed in the Samaritan ideal of Judaism: "What is hateful to you, do not do to your neighbor." The golden rule of Confucius is: "What you do not wish for yourself, do not impose on others" (Analects 12:2). The Christian version is: "In everything do to others as you would have them do to you; for this is the law and the prophets" (Matthew 7:12).

Hinduism and Buddhism also share this view, and go on to say that evil deeds will be punished, if not in this life then in the next—in other words, sin is its own punishment. Good deeds are correspondingly rewarded in this life or the next. When we show consideration for others, we are also showing consideration for ourselves, as we are all aspects of the same unity. In the words of the *Bhagavadgita,* "Seeing oneself in all and all in oneself, one does not injure others because that means injury to oneself." At the same time, one result of good deeds emphasized by Judaism, Hinduism, and other religions is that the whole world becomes a better place.

In religions there are ethics, moral codes, laws, and rules to guide us in our choice of good over evil. Confucianism takes this even further, with its many principles and laws on ethics and etiquette, all intended to result in harmony between our inner state of mind and our external behavior, when morally sound and true behavior will come to us naturally and spontaneously.

One Jewish tradition has it that the temple in Jerusalem was destroyed not because the people had sinned but because people had adhered too closely to the letter of the law. This may be interpreted to mean that morals, ethics, and laws are structures we require for as long as we are incomplete, but that if we develop active inner ethics based on compassion and humility we will no longer need these rules and principles. Taoism, Buddhism, and Hinduism all contain similar thoughts, and the Christian Meister Eckhart expressed this idea as well: "If you are righteous, then what you do will also be righteous."

The religions also stress that a person who has committed evil may make amends. Because we are incomplete, it is only human to err. True penance and repentance can eventually help us come to terms with those we have injured, with ourselves, and with the divine. Some religions describe this possibility of making up for our wrongdoings in notions like "divine grace" and "God's forgiveness."

## THE ULTIMATE JOY

The mystics describe the pleasure, the joy, and even the blessed state associated with the encounter between a human being and the divine. The brief rushes of happiness we may experience in our everyday lives are said to be nothing but a poor reflection, a pale image of the ultimate joy of an actual encounter with God. William James, a psychologist of religion, noted that "this sort of happiness in the absolute and everlasting is what we find nowhere but in religion." This is no instant of pleasure before life returns to normal, but an endless, timeless blessed state. Jesus spoke of it. Buddha and his enlightened successors referred to it. The

Hindu holy men bore witness to it. Muslim and Jewish mystics have described it. It is a kind of joy and peace that knows no end, in the meeting with the Absolute.

## AFTER DEATH

"Lend an ear, O monks! Deliverance from death has been found." These were said to be the first words of Buddha to his soon-to-be disciples when he had achieved enlightenment, and they highlight the key position, in Buddhism and many other religions, of the idea of death and what happens after death.

Mystical traditions share the belief that the divine in the human never dies. No matter whether it is called Atman, divine spark, or nirvana element, it does not die when the body ceases to function. This, however, is where the agreement ends. One of the strongest lines of demarcation between religions goes between the belief in reincarnation and the conviction that human beings live only one life in this world and are resurrected in another.

According to Hinduism and Buddhism, we are born and reborn time after time, until we are finally delivered and become one with moksha or nirvana. They see the deepest states of meditation as our opportunity to glimpse what awaits us on the other side. Correspondingly, some people's near-death experiences have been interpreted as real glimpses of the afterlife. At times, the Western world has regarded the thought of reincarnation with skepticism, although today it is more accepted. As Voltaire put it: "It is not more surprising to be born twice than once."

Neither Christianity nor Islam accepts the idea of reincarnation, since both see this life as our only life on earth. We are born to the world, we live our lives, and we die. What happens after that is something completely different. Judaism holds a more diffuse view of the afterlife, and so in Jewish mysticism both theories of reincarnation and claims that we only have one life on earth exist concomitantly. This open attitude is justified using the argument that it is meaningless to speculate about something of which we can never be sure, and what is important is the life we are living in the present. Baruch Spinoza, the Jewish philosopher and mystic, said, in a view not very different from that of Taoism, "A free man thinks of nothing less than of death; and his wisdom is a meditation not of death, but of life."

There are also widely differing views of what actually remains after death: Is it our soul, our personality, or could it even be our body? Or is all that is retained the part of consciousness we share with all human beings, the divine spark that once again becomes part of the great consciousness? While Buddhism and Taoism imply that what is left after death are some aspects of our consciousness that are separate from our personality, the monotheistic religions and Hinduism lean more toward the belief that our personalities are maintained on the other side of death.

## THE MESSAGE OF LOVE

Loving our neighbor is a basic notion in the major religions. This is expressed in monotheism in many ways, including these words from Leviticus that were later quoted by Jesus as part of the fundamental commandment for his disciples to follow: "You shall love your neighbor as yourself" (Leviticus 19:18; see also Mark 12:31). Hinduism even provides us with a motivation for loving others when it says, "You shall love your neighbor as yourselves because you are your neighbor, and mere illusion makes you believe that your neighbor is something different from yourselves." Buddha compared the compassion and love with which we should face our fellow human beings with the love of a mother for her child.

This is not only a matter of deeds, but also of feelings. The message of love covers not only our neighbor but all of humanity and, in its extension, all living things. Store is also set by other positive sentiments in relation to our fellow human beings, including compassion, empathy, tolerance, and forgiveness.

Greater love for our fellow human beings results, as a rule, in more good deeds, but not only that. The major religions all claim that love of our fellow human beings also leads to a deeper understanding of the fact that we are all fundamentally part of the same divine context. At the same time, we learn to love the divine and this allows us to experience divine love streaming back to ourselves. In the first letter of John we read that "Whoever does not love does not know God, for God is love" (4:8). This idea of love between God and humankind and between one human being and another is a theme and variations that is an inherent part of the fabric of the great religions.

## GOD'S HAND

Religions describe how people, in the course of their search, may experience events that are difficult if not impossible to explain. In some, religious experiences are described that temporarily violate the laws of nature. Events that are difficult to explain simply on the basis of random chance are even more common. Such an event or series of events may lead a person to find a whole new orientation in life, or provide new meaning to his or her life. The common denominator of all these experiences is that they are neither impossible nor in contravention of the laws of nature, but are certainly improbable. Often, but not always, they are experienced at times of crisis in a person's life. It is up to each individual to choose to take them in with a sense of wonder or gloss them over as random events.

Carl Gustav Jung approached such phenomena from a scientific angle, referring to them as "synchronicities." These may include premonitions that are fulfilled, emotional certainty about something happening to someone we hold dear, improbable but meaningful coincidences, and dreams that come true. Synchronicities are not a scientifically proven phenomena, but are commonly described by the religious and non-religious alike. In religion, these unexpected experiences are sometimes referred to as "God's hand." These phenomena do not by definition require laws of nature to be broken, but they do imply that there may be "principles" of nature we have not yet discovered.

## WISDOM

*In seeking wisdom thou art wise;*
*in imagining that thou hast attained it—thou art a fool.*
—Talmud

Religions assert that ultimate wisdom, like the divine, may be found at the core of every human being. A person who has accessed this internal treasure trove containing the divine also lives in wisdom. Religions stress that truly spiritual human beings can be recognized because they possess this quality.

Thus a human being may be guided by his or her inner voice. Some religions even assert that we may experience this internal guide as a personality, a leader inside us, referred to in Islam as *al-Khadir*, in Hinduism as *Paramatma*, and in Buddhism as the "inner spiritual guide."

Yet a great danger lurks in this idea, because a person's consciousness may give rise to voices other than that of wisdom. How can we be sure that it is the voice of wisdom speaking? According to most religions this is difficult to know, and therefore we must always be aware of the necessity to question these experiences. There are some points of guidance, one being that the voice of wisdom would not counsel us to injure another human being. Another is that inner wisdom does not speak out loudly and clearly, but addresses us softly and in hints rather than clear instructions. In order to hear it, we must hone our listening skills.

The Taoist term *tê* is an attempt to capture this inner wisdom. *Tê* implies acquiring the ability to do what is right by living in harmony with the hidden forces in the universe. If we strive neither for external nor internal success and behave without preconceived intentions, our actions will come to reflect wisdom.

Education, observation, contemplation, and encounters with others may make us more knowing individuals. During the course of our life journey we will have the opportunity to learn. However, according to religion we can only reach ultimate wisdom through contact with that which is divine inside us. As the Upanishads put it:

Two kinds of knowledge must be known, this is what all who
know Brahman tell us, the higher and the lower knowledge. . . .
The higher knowledge is that by which the Indestructible
(Brahman) is apprehended.

This ultimate wisdom will give us insight into what is in the hearts of our fellow human beings, to see reality as it actually is and to understand that which is truly important.

## THE WAY OF HUMANKIND

Religion holds that it is the great mission of every human being to strive within him- or herself for "wholeness" and greater awareness. This will enable us to unify, inside ourselves, human intellect with that which is beyond awareness, the divine. All human beings have this responsibility.

As a Jewish scholar once put it: "When I appear before the heavenly court, they will not ask me why I was not Moses. They will ask me why I was not myself."

When individuals have achieved the greatest truth, they have a double task. The first is to become a teacher for others and share their insights about the highest truths and the ways we may travel to reach them. The second is more difficult to put into words. The idea is that humanity is dependent on the existence of righteous individuals to preserve our world with their all-embracing love and compassion. Religions say that there are always and have always been such people, quietly accomplishing this task. There may be one in our immediate vicinity, who can be sure? If there is, he or she will simply stand out as a good person. It is also unclear how this task is passed down from one generation to the next, but the idea of "the righteous" can be found in Judaism, Islam, Christianity, and Hinduism. It is said that as long as there are such people on earth, we may go on living in security and without fear for the future.

## ✍ 17

## *Is It Important to Seek*
## *a Concealed God?*

Religions differ from one another in many respects, as expressed in their different traditions, rites, myths, social norms, laws, and ways of searching. They also have fundamental similarities, including the belief that a concealed, indescribable force is at the basis of everything. This highest reality is often referred to as "God," but may also have other names. This divine center contains, among others, the following themes:

+ God is an all-embracing force of which we are part, although we are often unaware of it.
+ God cannot be described in words, since language is insufficient for the purpose, but can only be experienced.
+ God may be experienced within us when we search in various ways, including meditation, prayer, and contemplation.
+ God is intimately intertwined with the concepts of "love," "goodness," and "wisdom."
+ Humankind needs God and, according to some schools of belief, this need is reciprocal.
+ There is a divine law of ethics.
+ We cannot achieve complete knowledge with our five senses and so all that we can experience through our intellect is but a pale imitation of "real reality," which is unity.

God is beyond our senses but can still be reached, religions tell us. We can intuit experiences that defy description, for example in love or in an intense nearness to nature. We may be astounded by the endlessly complex

structure of life and we may sense that there is some force governing creation. In difficult periods of our lives, when we suffer deeply, we may feel
there is a force guiding us forward: a motion so gentle that afterward we
may ask ourselves whether it really was there at all.

Because our conscious, rational minds cannot help us, we can only inti-
mate the whole rather than understand it. But religion teaches us that the
inner search, when we allow our intellect and our senses to become quiet,
can lead us to an intuitive experience of the deepest truths.

Our knowledge of life, the world, and the universe is increasing at
incredible speed. Questions that could only previously be answered by
referring to the existence of a God are now subject to "natural" explanations. At the same time, it is clear that the progress of science has neither
led to proof for nor against the existence of a concealed God. Science has
not yet been and may never be able to provide all the answers.

Taking the matter to its extreme, we can say that there are two (not
exclusive) explanatory models. Either God is a biochemical process in the
human brain, the function of which is to protect the intellect from experiencing the world as insecure and meaningless—feelings that could have
resulted in the downfall of the human race in an evolutionary perspective—or else there is a God.

## SOME BASIC QUESTIONS

Assuming that religions are correct in their assumption that the divine
does exist as a hidden, indescribable force in the universe, we may pose the
following central questions:

### Is the existence of God of any significance?

The indescribable God may be so hidden and so far beyond human contact that there is good reason to question the significance of the divine.
This force may be so enclosed in itself that its existence has no importance. One thought found in both Jewish and Christian mysticism is that
the *manifestations* of God are more important than the infinite God.

In spite of this possible self-sufficiency, most religious texts speak of
God as significant to humankind and to all of creation, which means that,
for religions, the significant questions are "how?" and "why?"

*Does God "want" anything of us and if so, what?*

The various religions address this issue of what is expected of humankind.
The answers they have given include:

+ to strive for goodness toward, compassion with, and love of our
  fellow human beings;
+ to try to achieve greater wisdom;
+ to seek the divine within ourselves.

If we assume that these central themes are more than social and moral
standards dressed in religious guise, we may sense a direction in which the
divine tries to lead humankind.

### *Where are we headed?*

The last few centuries have been a time of great development. Science and
industrial progress have altered a number of our assumptions and many
of the deepest secrets of life and the universe have been revealed. In addition to the positive effects of these steps forward in technology and the
natural sciences, the last few centuries have also seen a development in the
direction of democracy, tolerance, and human rights for more and more
people in our world. In many respects, the development is positive.

At the same time, many people in our world suffer. Although development has resulted in the possibility of building up a world in which starvation, disease, war, crime, and accidents are on the decline, the relatively
good conditions do not apply to all, and we are frequently reminded of
what human beings are capable of doing to one another. At the same time,
we may be in the process of destroying the earth, our home in the universe. Our environment is slowly being driven toward degradation.
Nuclear weapons and other instruments of mass destruction are being
manufactured and refined, often on the pretense that they safeguard
peace. In spite of the development of antibiotics and vaccines, our world
is still struck by sudden, new epidemics that devastate the populations of
large countries where the contagion is allowed to spread although more
could be done to prevent it. And poverty and starvation remain among
the major problems facing the world.

All the good sides of development are in competition with the destructive
forces that may be released by it. The phenomenal developments of recent

centuries also appear to have driven humanity toward inconceivable hazards with surprising consistency. In the words of Viktor Frankl: "Since Auschwitz we know what man is capable of. And since Hiroshima we know what is at stake."

Is it merely a coincidence that spirituality seems to be losing ground in large parts of the world at the same time, along with our sense of intimacy with all things and our relationship to the divine? The natural sciences and several of the major religions all put forward the idea that this world is neither the first nor the only of its kind. There may have been worlds before ours that were destroyed. If so, the question is why? Could it be the case that these worlds consistently developed a species that drove itself to its own fall? A species which, in parallel, developed in intelligence and lost in spirituality? If we believe this may have been the case, it is natural to go on to ask whether we are once again in the process of losing everything by letting the scale holding intellect weigh so much more than the scale holding spirituality.

### Can the search for God help us walk this tightrope between development and destruction?

Various religions claim that the answer to that question is yes, referring us to the human need for divine wisdom, inner counsel, and love. Each of us is the bearer of good and evil inside ourselves, which means that we have a choice. Religions hold that the divine in human beings is on the side of good.

We may, however, object that a multitude of evil deeds have been done in the name of God by human beings who claim to believe in and pray to God. This is the dark side of religion, the side in which our image of God reflects human aggression, pride, and hunger for power, an image of God that may provide a pretext for human evil. Religion teaches us that a human being who commits evil in the name of God can never be anywhere near the true God. At the same time, the concealed God we find in the different religions is a unifying force. If we are fundamentally unified by one and the same God, there is no justification for war or wrongdoings committed in the name of gods.

We need leadership that is not driven by a lust for power, by fundamentalist ideologies or personal gain, but by inner wisdom that will not lead us to start wars, to allow our fellow human beings to suffer, or to destroy our environment. The wisdom of religion is about seeing ourselves, humbly, in our fellow human beings and for this reason treating them as "human beings" in the deepest sense of the term. As Martin Buber put it: "When a man has made peace within himself, he will be able to make peace in the whole world."

*What would happen if all human beings began to live their lives compassionately, with love and inner wisdom?*

This utopian idea is found in many religions as an indication that we would then be in a position to create something entirely new for humankind, something better than we can even possibly imagine. God may not even have to exist for this to happen. It might suffice for more people to turn the light of their search inward, to learn to ask themselves the really important questions, sometimes in doubt, always in honesty. Perhaps that would be enough.

## IN CONCLUSION

This book is not an endeavor to offer definite answers. And so its concluding word can be no more than a "perhaps." Perhaps a concealed God underpins the universe. Perhaps God is there, in every living thing, representing the most important and best aspects of humankind, the capacity for wisdom, goodness, and love. Perhaps the divine gives meaning to our lives and perhaps there is a reality beyond the hubris of our reason and our senses.

There is not one single path to what we call God, but many. We may pursue our search using the road maps provided by Buddhism, Taoism, Hinduism, Islam, Judaism, or Christianity, or we can choose another route and still arrive at the destination. During the course of our journey and upon arrival we may, perhaps, find the answers for which humankind has such a deep desire.

I conclude with the words of two prominent spiritual thinkers:

God may be discerned in every thing and may be attained in every pure action. (Martin Buber)

For everything the understanding can grasp, and everything desire demands, is not God. Where understanding and desire have an end, there it is dark, there does God shine. (Meister Eckhart)

These words echo two themes central to the search for the innermost truths. One is the idea that God is both concealed and simultaneously omnipresent. The other is that only with utter humility and an awareness of our inability to fully understand may we approach the divine.

# ᔗ Select Bibliography

*Please note: Some of the books in the original bibliography do not exist in the English language and are therefore not included.*

## RELIGION

Armstrong, Karen. *History of God: The 4,000-Year Quest for Judaism, Christianity, and Islam.* New York: Ballantine Publishing Group, 1994.

Berger, Peter L. *A Rumor of Angels.* New York: Alfred A. Knopf, 1970.

Eliade, Mircea. *The Myth of the Eternal Return: Or Cosmos and History.* Princeton: Princeton University Press, 1971.

Heifetz, Harold. *Zen and Hasidism: The Similarities between Two Spiritual Disciplines.* Hoboken, NJ: Ktav Publishing House, 1996.

Küng, Hans. *Does God Exist? An Answer for Today.* New York: Crossroad, 1994.

Miles, Jack. *God: A Biography.* New York: Alfred A. Knopf, 1995.

Neiman, Carol and Emily Goldman. *Afterlife: The Complete Guide to Life After Death.* East Rutherford, NJ: Studio Books, 1994.

Parrinder, Geoffrey. *The World's Living Religions.* 1964.

Peterson, Michael, William Hasker, Bruce Reichenbach, and David Basinger. *Reason and Religious Belief.* New York: Oxford University Press, 1997.

Russell, Bertrand. *History of Western Philosophy.* New York: Simon & Schuster, 1945.

von Glasenapp, Helmuth. *Die fünf Weltreligionen.* Düsseldorf: Eugen Dietrichs Verlag, 1963.

Wilber, Ken. *A Brief History of Everything.* Boston: Shambhala Publications, 1996.

## MYSTICISM

Brunton, Paul. *The Secret Path.* York Beach, ME: Red Wheel, 1985.

———. *The Quest of the Overself.* York Beach, ME: Red Wheel, 1937.

Underhill, Evelyn. *Practical Mysticism.* Mineola, NY: Dover Publications, 2000.

Younghusband, Francis. *Modern Mystics.* Manchester, NH: Ayer Company Publishers, Inc., 1977.

## JUDAISM

Buber, Martin. *The Way of Man: According to the Teaching of Hasidism.* New York: Carol Publishing Group, 1995.

Gordis, Daniel. *God Was Not in the Fire.* New York: Simon & Schuster, 1997.

Ponce, Charles. *Kabbalah: An Introduction and Illumination for the World Today.* Wheaton: The Theosophical Publishing House, 1978.

Scholem, Gerschom. *Major Trends in Jewish Mysticism.* New York: Schocken Books, 1961.

Smith, Ronald Gregor. *Martin Buber.* Louisville: Westminster John Knox Press, 1967.

Steinberg, Milton. *Basic Judaism.* New York: Harcourt, 1965.

Steinsaltz, Adin. *The Essential Talmud.* Northvale, NJ: Jason Aronson Publishers, 1992.

## CHRISTIANITY

Anonymous. *The Cloud of Unknowning.* Harmondsworth: Penguin Books, 1976.

Clark, James M. *Meister Eckhart.* London: Thomas Nelson and Sons, 1957.

Egan, Harvey D. *Christian Mysticism: The Future of a Tradition.* Collegeville: Liturgical Press, 1992.

Johnston, William. *The Inner Eye of Love.* San Francisco: HarperSanFrancisco, 1978.

Lossky, Vladimir. *The Mystical Theology of the Eastern Church.* Crestwood, NY: St. Vladimir's Seminary Press, 1976.

Robinson, John A. T. *Honest to God.* Louisville: Westminster John Knox Press, 1963.

## ISLAM

Ernst, Carl W. *Shambhala Guide to Sufism.* Boston: Shambhala Publications, 1997.

Haeri, Shaykh Fadhlalla. *Sufism.* Chicago: Kazi Publications, 1996.

Nasr, S. H. *Living Sufism.* London: Unwin Paperbacks, 1980.

Nicholson, Reynold A. *The Mystics of Islam.* Chicago: Kazi Publications, 1996.

Shafii, Mohammad. *Freedom from the Self.* Chicago: Kazi Publications, 1996.

Shah, Indries. *The Way of the Sufi.* London: Octagon Press, 1983.

## HINDUISM

Eidlitz, Walther. *Krishna-Caitanya, Sein Leben und Sein Lehre.* Stockholm: Acta Universitatis Stockholmiensis, 1968.

Gandhi, Mahatma. *An Autobiography: The Story of My Experiments with Truth.* Mineola, NY: Dover Publications, 1983.

Nikhilananda, Swami. *Essence of Hinduism.* Boston: Beacon Press, 1948.

Radhakrishnan, Sarvepalli. *The Hindu View of Life.* San Francisco: HarperSanFrancisco, 1988.

## BUDDHISM

Boisselier, Jean. *The Wisdom of the Buddha.* New York: Harry N. Abrams, 1994.

Dalai Lama. *The Power of Compassion.* London: Thorsons, 1995.

Govinda, Lama Anagarika. *Buddhist Reflections.* York Beach, ME: Red Wheel, 1991.

Rinpoche, Sogyal. *The Tibetan Book of Living and Dying.* New York: Harper Collins, 1993.

Sayagyi U Ba Khin. *Dhamma Texts.* Heddington: The Sayagyi U Ba Khin Memorial Trust, 1985.

## TAOISM AND CONFUCIANISM

Cooper, Jean C. *Taoism: The Way of the Mystic.* Northamptonshire: The Aquarian Press, 1972.

Grigg, Ray. *The Tao of Being: A Think and Do Workbook.* Atlanta, GA: Humanics Publishing Group, 1989.

Legge, James. *Confucius: Confucian Analects, the Great Learning, and the Doctrine of the Mean.* Mineola, NY: Dover Publications, 1971.

## NATURAL SCIENCE AND RELIGION

Capra, F. *The Tao of Physics.* Boston: Shambhala Publications, 1991.

Davies, Paul. *The Mind of God: The Scientific Basis for a Rational World.* New York: Simon & Schuster, 1992.

————. *The Cosmic Blueprint*. New York: Simon & Schuster, 1988.

Einstein, Albert. *The World as I See It*. New York: Philosophical Library, Inc., 1958.

Gell-Mann, Murray. *The Quark and the Jaguar: Adventures in the Simple and the Complex*. New York: W. H. Freeman & Co., 1994.

Hawking, Stephen. *A Brief History of Time*. New York: Bantam Books, 1988.

————. *Black Holes and Baby Universes and Other Essays*. New York: Bantam Books, 1993.

Tipler, Frank. *The Physics of Immortality: Modern Cosmology, God, and the Resurrection of the Dead*. New York: Doubleday, 1996.

Zukav, Gary. *The Dancing Wu Li Masters*. New York: Harper Trade, 1979.

## PSYCHOLOGY AND RELIGION

Frankl, Viktor E. *Man's Search for Meaning*. Boston: Beacon Press, 1963.

Freud, Sigmund. *The Future of an Illusion*. New York: W. W. Norton, 1975.

Gay, Peter. *Freud: A Life for Our Time*. New York: W. W. Norton, 1988.

Jacobi, Jolande. *Psychology of C. G. Jung*. New Haven: Yale University Press, 1973.

James, William. *Varieties of Religious Experience*. New York: NAL, 1958.

Jung, Carl Gustav. *Memories, Dreams, Reflections*. New York: Pantheon Books, 1963.

————. *Man and His Symbols*. New York: Doubleday, 1969.

Stevens, Anthony. *On Jung*. Princeton: Princeton University Press, 1999.

# ∼ Index of Names